"*A Noble Quest: Cultiv____ ____ ____ ____ ____ Adolescents* by Dr. Arthur D. ____ ____ ____ ____ tool for the spiritual development of today's adolescent. One will j____ linkage between the sacred and the secular in the process of cultivating spirituality in youth and young adults becoming totally Christian and fully human. A Noble Quest will enhance both understanding and skill for the spiritual leader of young people today."

**Rev. Jeremiah J. Cullinane, D.Min.**
*Professor of Theology & Ministry*
*Silver Lake College of the Holy Family*
*(Manitowoc, Wisconsin)*

"*Anyone who is seriously engaged in the quest to discern the movements of adolescent spirituality within the church will find this amazing book to be theologically informed, pastoral in approach, and a practical guide. Dr. Canales presents the best of the literature in a style that is clear and concise, offering profound and sometimes challenging insights, a must-read for anyone who serves our youth.*"

**Rev. David B. Beaudry, M.A., Pastor**
*Holy Spirit Catholic Church*
*(Kimberly, Wisconsin)*

"Insightful, relevant, formative, and transformative; all Catholic youth ministers need to make room on their resource shelf for Canales' **A Noble Quest**. It is a much needed resource that will serve to enhance the spiritual journey of young people as well as those who are called to minister to youth."

**Len DiPaul, Ed.D.**
*Director, Pastoral and Theological Studies*
*Neumann University*
*(Aston, Pennsylvania)*

"Dr. Arthur D. Canales' book, **A Noble Quest: Cultivating Spirituality in Catholic Adolescents**, adds to the wealth of resources serving Catholic youth ministry leaders by focusing on the spiritual life of the adolescent. Unlike many books that begin with the ministry, A Noble Quest starts with the young person and focuses on *the faith journey of the adolescent from a variety of perspectives. This book brings together research, vision, theory, and practice, providing practical ways to integrate spiritual practices within youth ministry. This is a go-to resource for all who work with youth and all who seek to invite young people on a noble quest of responding in faith to the call of our loving God."*

**Tom East, M.A.**
*Director, Center for Ministry Development*
*(Gig Harbor, Washington)*
*Author of* Leadership for Catholic Youth Ministry

*"With clear focus and intent, Dr. Art Canales sets out on his own 'noble quest' to support each of us as we labor 'to enhance and strengthen Christian spirituality in Catholic young people.' It is a challenging and comprehensive resource for adults engaged in the lives of young Catholics negotiating the often complicated stage of life called adolescence.*

*Grounded in good developmental psychology, an extensive reflection on the nature of spirituality, a synthesis of ecclesial documents concerning youth ministry, and the reality of American life today, Art provides a solid basis for developing a Catholic adolescent spirituality. The author sets this spirituality squarely in the context of an Incarnational Sacramentality lived out in the larger context of Catholic Youth Ministry.*

*After exploring ways to strengthen Eucharist spirituality in Catholic adolescents, the author explores 'Twelve Pastoral Practices' that help cultivate spirituality in Catholic adolescents. The 'twelve,' as Art develops them, and a more in-depth exploration of 'three spiritual practices' (meditation, contemplation, and spiritual direction), provide a compendium of action and reflective practices that will move a young person through adolescence into a truly adult Catholicism. His book provides adults with concrete direction for working with these various pastoral practices.*

*The book concludes with a realistic assessment of the strengths and limitations of the pastoral practice of cultivating adolescent spirituality in Catholic youth ministry settings. A Noble Quest is theoretical and practical, theological and pastoral, as well as idealistic and* realistic. Dr. Canales' book makes an important contribution to the world of pastoral theology and youth ministry."

**Rev. Louis T. Brusatti, D.Min.**
*Dean of the School of Humanities*
*Professor of Religious Studies and Theological Studies*
*Saint Edward's University (Austin, Texas)*

"The book by Dr. Art Canales, ***A Noble Quest: Cultivating Spirituality in Catholic Adolescents***, should be recommended reading for all youth ministry leaders! The book attempts and succeeds to connect adolescent spiritual development within a comprehensive youth ministry framework. Art brings together the documents on Catholic youth ministry, with key texts from the past thirty years that have informed Catholic adolescent spirituality, and findings from the National Study of Youth and Religion, to offer a blueprint for parents, youth ministry leaders, religious educators, and the entire parish community acting as the support framework necessary to cultivate adolescent spirituality today."

**Kevin Prevou, M.A.**
*Director of Youth and Young Adult Ministry*
*Diocese of Fort Worth, Texas*

"***A Noble Quest: Cultivating Spirituality in Catholic Adolescents*** is an indispensable resource for adults who minister and pray with youth. Writing with an experienced and modern approach to understanding adolescents, Dr. Art Canales bridges the mystery between adolescent culture and Catholic teen spirituality. With defining insights on adolescent development and ministerial perspectives on aiding teens in today's culture, this resource is an important tool for every youth leader, parent, and priest."

**Tommy Sustaita**
*Director of Youth Ministry*
*Saint Louis Catholic Church (Austin, Texas)*

"As a long-time Catholic educator and minister, it is apparent to me that we are a Church in crisis, particularly in failing to meet teens where they are at in an authentic manner. ***A Noble Quest:***

*Cultivating Spirituality in Catholic Adolescents* fills a much needed void in Catholic adolescent formation. This book is thorough, engaging, informative, supportive, and challenging – quite an achievement while being concise! From classical theology and adolescent psychology, to the latest youth-ministry research and current adolescent cultural trends, Canales does a remarkable job of informing the reader and calling us, the Church, to action in ministering to our youth and youth leaders. Drawing from numerous, well-respected sources, Canales paints a broad picture which illustrates the richness of the Catholic Tradition, while simultaneously highlighting the dire need for full-time youth ministries with well-educated leaders who facilitate teens in embracing that richness of Tradition. This book serves as both a resource and a challenge to anyone who has a heart for the youth of our Church, and it offers practical tools to engage today's teens along with the theology to support it."

**Paul C. Griffith, M.A.**
*Religion Teacher*
*Central Catholic High School (Portland, Oregon)*

"FINALLY… a solid youth ministry resource that is both informative and motivational! **A Noble Quest** combines cutting-edge research and current statistics with the timeless guidance of Church documents to formulate practical solutions for one of the major challenges of Catholic youth ministry, namely plugging youth into the transformational power of Catholic spirituality. Dr. Canales is able to use his experience in youth ministry to move us from theory to practice, from inspiration to application, to challenge and equip us to lead youth closer to Christ and His Church. This is a must-have resource for all youth ministers and campus ministers who are serious about awakening and renewing the young Church. When I finished this book it reminded me of the reasons I got into youth ministry in the first place!"

**Doug Weisbruch**
*Director of Youth & Young Adult Ministry*
*Saint Luke Catholic Church (Temple, Texas)*

"**A Noble Quest** is informative, practical, and empowering! Dr. Canales presents a relevant approach to today's adolescents. Drawing upon extensive research and experience, ***A Noble Quest*** equips the reader to better understand and serve the great spiritual needs of our young church. Furthermore, the book is formatted to be a catechetical tool for your ministry team with discussion questions as well as practical suggestions. If you are seeking to make a difference where it matters most with adolescents, A Noble Quest should top your reading list!"

**Chris Bartlett, M.A.**
*Director of Youth and Young Adult Ministry,*
*Diocese of Austin, Texas*

"Dr. Canales work is a well conceived document of the understanding of Catholic adolescent spirituality as well as an excellent tool for youth ministers and all concerned with Catholic youth. This book is ready to use in the modern practical development of spirituality in Catholic teenagers. Using both a historic eye regarding adolescent spiritual development, as well as a keen understanding of modern techniques and paradigms, Canales sets before the field a useful, practical and spirit-driven work in ***A Noble Quest*** that should be read by all who minister to and with Catholic youth. Both youth and those who serve them will receive great benefit and spiritual strengthening from this master work, as the text provides uniquely rich food for the "interiority" of the youth minister, who may then in turn serve "exteriorly" young people in their respective ministerial care. This is a must have and must read tome for anyone interested in adolescent Catholic Spirituality."

**Ron Landfair, M.A.**
*Director of Multicultural Evangelization,*
*Diocese of Lansing, Michigan*
*NFCYM Board of Directors Member*

"Adolescent lives have never been more challenging... a beacon of hope is to 'grasp' tightly to those resources that feed their hunger for a meaningful spiritual life. **A NOBLE QUEST: Cultivating Spirituality in Catholic Adolescents** is not another reinvention of the wheel; instead Canales incorporates timeless spiritual practices into one valuable *resource for those working with young people. The discussion questions at the end of each chapter draw the reader into reflection of their own spirituality thus inspiring the importance to guide adolescents to seek the deeper Truth. This is a must read for all Catholic youth workers... indeed a noble quest!"*

**Diana Pisana, M.A.**
*Associate Director of Youth Ministry,
Diocese of Little Rock, Arkansas*

*A Noble Quest: Cultivating Spirituality in Catholic Adolescents*
Copyright © 2011 by Arthur Canales

All rights reserved
Printed in the United States of America

No part of this book may be reproduced or transmitted in any form or by any means, electronic or mechanical, including photocopying and recording, or by an information storage and retrieval system, without permission in writing from the authors.

ISBN: 978-1-936417-35-3

Published by PCG Legacy,
a division of Pilot Communications Group, Inc.
317 Appaloosa Trail Waco, TX 76712
www.pilotcomgroup.com/pcglegacy

HOW TO REACH THE AUTHOR:
artcanales@yahoo.com

# A NOBLE QUEST

*Cultivating Spirituality in Catholic Adolescents*

**ARTHUR DAVID CANALES**
FOREWORD BY ROBERT J. MCCARTY

# A Noble Quest

# Dedication

To the lovely ladies in my life:

*Anna Catherine & Tanya Michelle & Elida Luna*

And especially to . . .

All the over-worked and under-paid Catholic youth ministers who tirelessly and faithfully stand by, with, and for Catholic adolescents, and who assist Catholic young people on their noble quest toward a deeper and more meaningful spiritual life.

# A Noble Quest

# TABLE OF CONTENTS

| | |
|---|---:|
| **Dedication** | 11 |
| **Foreword** | 15 |
| **Introduction** | 21 |
| **Chapter 1**: Approaching Adolescents | 27 |
| **Chapter 2**: Defining, Describing, and Situating Catholic Adolescent Spirituality | 47 |
| **Chapter 3**: Strengthening Eucharistic Spirituality in Catholic Adolescents | 67 |
| **Chapter 4**: The Usefulness of 12 Pastoral Practices for Cultivating Spirituality in Catholic Adolescents | 81 |
| **Chapter 5**: Three Appropriate Spiritual Practices for Cultivating Catholic Adolescent Spirituality | 101 |
| **Chapter 6**: Strengths and Limitations of the Pastoral Practices of Cultivating Adolescent Spirituality in Catholic Youth Ministry Settings | 129 |
| **Conclusion** | 141 |
| **Bibliography** | 144 |
| **Endnotes** | 152 |
| **About the Author** | 158 |

A Noble Quest

# FOREWORD

I thoroughly like this book and its title — it challenges and inspires — and looking at our ministry with young people as a "noble quest" certainly captures my imagination. Dr. Art Canales offers an insightful description of the territory of adolescents today, both in the Church and civic arena, and then provides a challenging map for effectively fostering their spirituality. This combination of scholarly analysis and practical strategies makes *A Noble Quest: Cultivating Spirituality in Catholic Adolescents* a valuable resource for all those engaged with the young Church.

To provide an additional lens to this endeavor, I want to suggest several characteristics of millennial spirituality which I believe are infused throughout this book as a way of further highlighting Art's contribution to comprehensive Catholic youth ministry. The term "millennial" refers to those young people born between 1982 and 2002, which now includes our middle school and high school adolescents, as well as most of our current young adults.

## Spirituality of the Millennial Generation

We must be clear to state that the Millennial Generation is different from any previous generation. We are familiar with the old rationalizations about this stage of life: it's normal for young people to leave the church during young adulthood only to return when they marry and want their children to have the sacraments. After all, that's what many of us did. However, this pattern is no longer true for many young people. The world is changing so rapidly for today's young people that there are no 'normal' patterns. Technology, computers, the media, and the globalization of economy have created a brand new world and the Millennial Generation will be the first to grow up in and be totally immersed as citizens of this world. They don't know of any other world.

Many young people today are searching for an authentic experience of God. According to a 1998 Gallup Study, one in three teenagers by age sixteen reports a significant, personal experience of God. A 2006 report characterized young people as leading a spiritual renewal in our country. Young people need a faith that enables them to better articulate their experience of God. They want a religion that helps them understand life with its joys and sufferings. They search for a faith that makes sense, that provides direction and meaning, and that challenges. And they want to be connected with others who are on this same search. Gallup's finding raises two significant questions: (1) do young people have the language to express and talk about that experience and (2) do teenagers feel connected to a faith community where they can share that experience and integrate that experience into their lives. This nexus of spiritual experiences, religious language and faith community has serious implications for youth ministry and adolescent faith formation.

There are several identifiable characteristics of the millennial spirituality, which I firmly believe that Canales addresses and offers insights about. There is no doubt that adolescent spirituality is important. For the millennial, the emphasis, though, is on the spiritual journey, rather than on organized religion. This journey is complete with questions, doubts, and a need to grapple with faith questions with peers and with believing adults. Today's young people want to share their spiritual journey with others, but with others who are experienced as supportive, welcoming, authentic, and caring. The focus on this journey is on discipleship versus membership. Today's Catholic teenagers are more interested in the parish "out there," focused on involvement in the world, rather than in the parish "in here," focused on internal theological and church issues.

# Foreword

Increasingly, the Millennial Generation are believers, not belongers. If youth choose to belong to a faith community, their decision is often based on the ways they are welcomed and engaged by the community: vibrant worship, discipleship, service and social justice, and pastoral outreach, rather than based on theology or doctrine. This is the reason that *A Noble Quest* is so valuable to comprehensive Catholic youth ministry because it addresses these spiritual issues and provides insightful pastoral strategies to engage adolescents both in contemporary and traditional Catholic spirituality and spiritual practices.

Young people are open to transcendence, mystery, beauty, compassion, inclusivity, and justice. They see spirituality as about withdrawal from the rat-race, competition, hatred, judgementalism, and the violence they experience in society. However, youth often see religion as about judgment, elitism, abstract doctrine, boring rituals, and strict boundaries and rules. Our young people often hear more about what we *do not* believe and *cannot do*, rather than what we *do* believe and must do. Unfortunately, so few young people associate Catholicism with spirituality, and the ministry challenge is to reconstruct Catholicism for a new generation. Art Canales accomplishes this task in this new, challenging, informational, and inspiring book!

Millennials are drawn to the Jesus who *understands* their suffering, rather than to the Boomers' Jesus who wants to be their best friend; however, the one who is speaking of Jesus has to be experienced as supportive and caring. Millennials are attracted to an individual relationship with Jesus. The youth ministry challenge is to connect their vertical spirituality, "me and Jesus," with the horizontal, "me/we and Jesus" of the larger parish, diocesan, regional, and universal community. An adolescent's experience of Church is critical, if the message is to have any meaning. The young people who stay connected to Church are those in relationship with the pastor, youth minister, or other key adults, those who feel welcomed, and those who experience a sense of home. If no one in the parish talks to them, they will simply leave.

Young people desire to experience the transcendence and power of God. They need spiritual experiences and a spiritual context. Young people are attracted to the experience of national and international gatherings, sponsored by the Catholic Church. But they need the local context that provides opportunities to reflect upon their experiences and to integrate their learnings into their daily life. The parish can be the natural context. Moreover, teenagers desire a real and personal experience of faith versus a virtual reality. The use of all the arts and nature to discover God, e.g. video, dance, music, sculpture, and art, will be necessary to heal the sacred/secular split. Their need for sensorial experiences and powerful symbols, beyond words and cognitive literacy, will have a major impact on the ways we minister and worship as Church. Throughout, *A Noble Quest*, Canales offers such insights that intersect young people with tangible spiritual activities.

## Ministry Challenges

Given this description of the "territory," there are several elements that are essential for the ministry "map" in this new millennium. Consequently, though, this is a map that is still under construction. Proclaim the Good News . . . and proclaim it again and again! Young people need to hear Jesus' message of the Reign of God and they need to hear our faith stories and Traditions. Young people can be challenged to see the world through the lens of faith and begin to differentiate between the societal dream and the Jesus dream. Teenagers, indeed, are hungry for a dream that captures their imagination. The Church needs to be *countercultural*, renewing our emphasis on social justice and creating a noble adventure that responds to young people's desire to serve and make a difference in the world. Ah . . . and it is this noble adventure that is captured and articulated in *A Noble Quest*, which equips youth ministers and adolescents with the necessary spiritual activities and strategies to become countercultural in the world.

***Connect*** young people to the life of the faith community. Young people have a need to belong to something bigger than themselves, they have a need and a right to responsible participation in the faith community through participation in the liturgical, pastoral, and leadership ministries of the parish. Youth deserve to be connected to faith-filled adult role models and they need to use their gifts on behalf of the community. Teens need a place where they can ask their questions, express their doubts, and live out their convictions.

*Challenge* our young people to become disciples. Youth ministry must challenge young people to be followers of Jesus and active participants in building the Reign of God. They need to enter into a relationship with Jesus. Youth want to be committed, they want to be aligned with a community of committed believers, and they want to live out this commitment as authentic Christian disciples.

*Create* and construct opportunities for young people to serve. Adolescents have done extraordinary things for their community through service and outreach. Not only does their idealism and almost boundless energy enable them to "tackle" very difficult issues, but in the process, they increase their self esteem, confidence, enduring belief in the value of service, and their empathy and compassion for others in need. Youth begin to develop the values of the Reign of God through helping other and through service initiatives.

*Collaborate* with those institutions that can communicate value and caring. The popular African proverb reminds us that, "It takes an entire village to raise a child." The Church must collaborate with the rest of the village: the parents, schools, the social service agencies, and community organizations, so that not only is our ministry to, with, and for young people more effective, but also so that the Church is experienced as connected to and involved in the world.

## Conclusion

George Gallup, in a recent report, states: "The challenge to the churches is to build up their youth programs and put young people in places where they can challenge, disagree, and build up trust. If the world in (this new) century is going to be less sexist, less racist, less polluted, and more peaceful, we can thank our young people." This excellent resource — *A Noble Quest* — for Catholic youth ministry strongly suggests that Art Canales does concur. If the Church in this century is going to be more inclusive, more creative in our prayer and worship, more committed to justice and service, centered on Eucharist, and guided by committed and competent ordained and lay ministers, we can thank our young people.

— **Robert J. McCarty,** D.Min., Executive Director
National Federation for Catholic Youth Ministry
Washington, DC

# INTRODUCTION

*"This is what is needed: a Church for young people, which will know how to speak to their heart and enkindle, comfort, and inspire enthusiasm in it with the joy of the Gospel and the strength of the Eucharist; a Church which will know how to invite and to welcome the person who seeks a purpose for which to commit his whole existence; a Church which is not afraid to require much, after having given much; which does not fear asking from young people the effort of a noble and authentic adventure, such as that of the following of the Gospel."*[1]

**Pope John Paul II**
*1995, World Day of Prayer for Vocations*

The purpose of this book is to assist Catholic parents, adult leaders/catechists of youth ministry, parish youth ministers, diocesan directors of youth ministry, priests, and bishops in their noble quest of ministering to, for, and with Catholic adolescents on their journey of living the Catholic faith. Indeed, cultivating Christian spirituality in Catholic adolescents is a noble quest and is worthy of exploration and time. Some of the material contained in this book is a collection, reworking, and nuancing of three essays that I have previously written for academic journals.[2] The overarching goal of this book is to help adults to cultivate the spirituality in Catholic young people. Although this book might be a bit focused and cerebral at times, it should not discourage anyone from reading the book, and it is definitely not over anyone's head. The book is intended to guide adults-parents and those who work directly with adolescents-to integrate and implement its ideas and practices in order to enhance and strengthen Christian spirituality in Catholic young people.

In addition, it must be noted that this book is faithful to the two U.S. watershed documents pertaining to Catholic youth ministry: *A Vision of Youth Ministry* (1976) and *Renewing the Vision: A Framework for Catholic Youth Ministry* (1997). Both documents have been instrumental in helping shape and guide Catholic youth ministry in the United States of America. Moreover, both documents only address adolescent spiritual awareness and development through the themes and components of comprehensive Catholic youth ministry and do not specifically address adolescent spirituality in particular. This should not alarm the reader because both the *A Vision of Youth Ministry* and *Renewing the Vision* are guidelines for church youth workers to understand and utilize in their ministering to Catholic teenagers, and not hard and fast rules to follow or pastoral strategies to implement. Pastoral practices that enhance adolescent spirituality are typically derived through experience of youth ministers in the field and youth ministry educators.

## Why this book?

Spirituality is extremely important for adolescent development and has traditionally not been addressed specifically or the topic has merely been glossed over for many years. However, in the past five to ten years, articles on adolescent spirituality have appeared around the world in various academic journals and in national studies. As Catholics, spirituality is part and parcel of who we are. In general, people are stimulated by the sacred in various ways, and Christian spirituality ideally opens a person's mind and heart to experience the God. The Church has a responsibility to help foster a keener sense of spirituality and self-awareness of God through Jesus the Christ, but the ultimate burden of becoming more spiritually aware rests with each individual Christian. The life of a person must be moved to encounter the risen Christ and motivated by the Holy Spirit toward living the Christian life, and this is one of my hopes for this book: to help parents and youth workers move and motivate adolescents to a deeper and more fulfilling Catholic spiritual life.

## What is Catholic adolescent spirituality?

Although this question will be answered in detail throughout the book, the phrase *Catholic adolescent spirituality* is both difficult to pinpoint and is a rather nebulous term. Spirituality has so many different meanings and interpretations that it differs from person to person. It makes sense, then, that part of spirituality is captured in the human spirit because the human spirit is created in the divine image or *imago Dei* (image of God). The human spirit seems to allocate an internal and intuitive foundation for the human experience. Christian spirituality is formed by the interpersonal relationships that a Christian forms within the community of faith and the daily routine of a lived expression that centers around Jesus the Christ, the fountain of all Christian spirituality, and the self-communication and self-transcending compassion and mercy of God. In simpler words, Christian spirituality is the practice of the Christian faith, or living the actions that compose the Christian faith. When the great German Jesuit theologian Karl Rahner (1900-1980) was asked to respond to the question, why are you a Christian? Rahner's reply (1992) was simple: "I would like to be a Christian. . . . In the Christian view, one must in the end leave it to God to decide whether one really is-in theory and, above all, in practice-what one claims to be" (p. 3). "Saint Karl," as I like to call him, is simply suggesting that Christian spirituality is a process of becoming Christian and is a journey that will last a lifetime. Moreover, he suggests that Christian spirituality is concerned with doing and cultivating spirituality. Hence, a good broad and beginning definition for *Catholic adolescent spirituality* in this book will be ***a journey and a process of discovering God through the impact of a Catholic faith-life and the experience of a*** *teenage worldview.* In other words, Catholic adolescent spirituality will be a process in which young people enter into an encounter in Catholic activities, programs, and events. However, I must caution the reader that this broad definition will be further nuanced and more focused as the book unfolds.

In this book, each chapter addresses several ways to help the typical U.S. Catholic teenagers become more spiritually attuned to God. In addition, each chapter offers various pastoral strategies to help integrate spirituality into the lives of Catholic young people. I hope and pray that each reader finds theological answers to questions concerning adolescent spirituality and practical guidelines to help infuse spirituality into the lives of Catholic teenagers.

This book has been a labor of love and a journey in faith and patience. I began being interested in adolescent spirituality in 2000, but I did not begin to put "pen to paper" on the topic until 2005. Since 2005, I have written numerous articles on Catholic youth ministry and adolescent spirituality as well as having spent countless hours researching and pondering the topics. I have also been fortunate to travel across the country and discuss and teach about issues relating to Catholic adolescent spirituality to parish youth ministers and diocesan directors of youth ministry.

Like all projects, there are a few people behind the scenes that allow for the "show" to be a success, and this is true for this book as well. I want to express a special thanks to the many people who wrote endorsements for this work: Chris Bartlett, Rev. David B. Beaudry, Rev. Louis T. Brusatti, Rev. Jeremiah J. Cullinane, Len DiPaul, Thomas East, Ron Landfair, Paul C. Griffith, Diana Pisana, Kevin Prevou, Tommy Sustaita, and Doug Weisbruch. Each of these endorsements represents the wide varieties of ministers that stand to, for, and with young people in the church today, including pastors, theologians, adolescent specialists, parish youth ministers, diocesan directors of youth ministry, and high school theology teachers. I also would like to acknowledge two friends and professional colleagues for their support and encouragement in all my youth

# Introduction

ministry endeavors: The Most Reverend Gregory M. Aymond, Archbishop of New Orleans, whom I have much admiration and affection for and Robert J. McCarty, Executive Director, National Federation for Catholic Youth Ministry who wrote the Forward of this book.

This book is titled *A Noble Quest: Cultivating Spirituality in Catholic Adolescents*, and for good reason. The work that youth ministers embark upon is some of the most challenging and exciting ministry in the Catholic Church today. For adults to help young people journey toward a deeper and more meaningful spirituality is a noble quest.

Feast Day of Saint Aloysius Liguori Gonzaga<br>
Patron Saint of Youth<br>
June 21

# A Noble Quest

## CHAPTER ONE

# APPROACHING ADOLESCENTS

*"The young are in character prone to desire and ready to carry any desire they may have formed into action. Of bodily desires it is the sexual to which they are most disposed to give way, and in regard to sexual desire they exercise no self-restraint. They are changeful, too, and fickle in their desires, which are as transitory as they are vehement; for their wishes are keen without being permanent, like a sick [person 's] fits of hunger and thirst. [Adolescents] are passionate, irascible, and apt to be carried away by their impulses. They are the slaves, too, of their passion, as their ambition prevents their ever brooking a slight and renders them indignant at the mere idea of enduring an injury. [Teenagers] are charitable rather than the reverse, as they have never yet been witness of many villainies; and they are trustful, as they have not yet been often deceived. They are sanguine, too, for the young are heated by nature as drunken [people] by wine, not to say that they have not yet experienced frequent failures. Their lives are lived principally in hope. They have high aspirations; for they have never yet been humiliated by the experience of life, but are*

*unacquainted with the limiting force of circumstances. Youth is the age when people are most devoted to their friends, as they are then extremely fond of social intercourse. If the young commit a fault, it is always on the side of excess and exaggeration, for they carry everything too far, whether it be their love or hatred or anything else. Finally, they are fond of laughter and consequently facetious, facetiousness being disciplined insolence."*[3]

**Aristotle of Athens**
*4th Century B.C.E.*

The above quote should not be of any great surprise for those who work with adolescents on a regular basis. For good or for ill, it is quite remarkable that teenage issues have not changed significantly, nor have adolescents as a sub-group of people or as a sub-culture changed in the last 2,500 years. Developmentally, psychologically, socially, and perhaps spiritually, youth have expressed the same disposition and temperament with little modifications in identity formation and self, whether they are Christians or non-Christians.

This chapter will provide a deeper understanding of adolescents and help the reader to better discern adolescent behavior, identity, developmental theories, culture, and spirituality. Adolescence is a vast area of study, reaching out into various sub-branches; therefore, this chapter will give only the briefest description of the life and lore of adolescents with a twofold lens: (1) situating adolescents in the United States of America and (2) addressing adolescent issues in contemporary culture as a backdrop to assist youth ministers and high school campus ministers in discerning the complexities of adolescent life and behavior. Since there is an enormous amount of material written about adolescents, the focus of this chapter is to give youth ministers some important information concerning young people. The purpose of this discussion is to equip youth workers with certain knowledge regarding adolescents that will help them relate to the needs of young people more effectively and appropriately. It is that undercurrent that will lead the reader to a deeper understanding of the period of adolescence, as well as appreciate adolescent behavior.

## Defining Adolescence

In today's fast-paced society, adolescents seem to be moving faster than ever before. Considering Aristotle's description of young people, it may appear that teenagers during antiquity shared similar characteristics with teenagers today in U.S. society. Therefore, it is important that a working definition of adolescence emerge in order to help situate a keener comprehension concerning adolescents. The term "adolescents" represents a group of people-young people, juveniles, youth, and teenagers-youth ministers are called to minister to this particular population. The word "adolescence" refers to a phase or period of life that concentrates on biological, psychological, physiological, and sociological changes occurring in the life of a young person. According to developmental psychologist Richard M. Lerner (2002), "Adolescence is a period of transition, one when the biological, psychological, and social characteristics typical in children change in an integrated manner to become the biological, psychological, and social characteristics typical of adults" (p. 5). The period of teenage life typically begins with pubertal changes, which may be the most visible and universal features of this stage of growth.

The Catholic Jesuit psychologist Charles M. Shelton (1983), who has written most extensively on adolescent development and spirituality, maintains that the period of adolescence, as defined by the American Psychiatric Association, is as follows:

> A chronological period beginning with physical and emotional processes leading to sexual and psychosocial maturity and ending at an ill-defined time when the individual achieves independence and social productivity. The period is associated

with rapid physical, psychological, and social changes. (p. 2)

The critical phrase in the above definition that most defines adulthood in the United States is: *achieves independence and social productivity*. Therefore, it is usually not until the persons are beyond college that they achieve total emotional and financial independence from their parents. It is quite possible, then, that the period of adolescence may span at least ten years or more. For the purposes of this discussion, adolescence will be categorized as beginning with puberty and ending with completion of undergraduate education, a span of eleven years representing the approximate ages of 11-22. Granted, this discussion focuses on teenagers in the United States. Clearly, not all cultures around the world experience an extended time of adolescence like the U.S. culture enjoys. This is primarily in response to the increased training or education that is needed in adult life in this country.

## Periods of Adolescence

According to Shelton, the period known as adolescence has three developmental stages. These three periods are generally referred to as early adolescence, middle adolescence, and late adolescence. Therefore, it is helpful to briefly discuss these three periods of adolescent life.

*1. Early Adolescence*

The initial or first stage is referred to as *early adolescence* and is most commonly associated and identified with puberty (Shelton, 3). Generally, early adolescence encompasses the years from age 11 to 14, the typical junior high or middle school years. On a physical level, early adolescents are beginning to notice the change in their bodies. For boys, there are height spurts, early voice changes, the beginning growth of the penis, testes, scrotum, and pubic hair (Rice and Dolgin, p. 90). For girls, height spurts begin, along with slight growth of public hair, breasts, nipples, and usually get their first menstrual cycle (Rice and

Dolgin, p. 90). On an intellectual level, early adolescents are beginning to develop a limited propensity and capacity for creative thought, critical thinking, and introspection, but particularly in four areas related to verbal intelligence, numeric intelligence, reasoning, and spatial ability (Lerner, p. 85). On an emotional level, early adolescents are subject to erratic behavior and various mood expressions. They become anxious about fears and doubts because adolescents are seeking autonomy, but at the same time they still have major emotional attachment to their parents (Rice and Dolgin, pp. 236-237).

### 2. Middle Adolescence

The center period or second stage of adolescent development-the focus of this book-is referred to as *middle adolescence* and is most commonly related with the high school years (Shelton, p. 3). Typically, middle adolescence encompasses the years from age 15 to 18, the typical senior high school years, that is, ninth through twelfth grades.

On a physical level, middle adolescents are beginning to recognize they are emerging adults because their bodies are taking on new physical dimensions. For males, there is rapid development of body parts; this is the age of maximum physical growth; and beginning growth of auxiliary hair on legs, buttocks, and chest (Rice and Dolgin, p. 90). For adolescent females, there is a slight deepening of the voice; rapid growth of womanly body parts and is also the age of maximum growth (Rice and Dolgin, p. 91).

On an intellectual level, middle adolescents are developing formal operations such as the ability to think hypothetically, counterfactually, and propositionally; beginning to have a deeper sense of self and developing personal beliefs that may differ from their parents' beliefs; this is also a time when teenagers acquire *sarcasm* (an ironic reproach or a contemptuous remark) and *deception* (the fraudulent act or trick done deliberately). Middle adolescence is also a period when *equilibration*, that is, the process of reaching a balanced *assimilation* (whereby the adolescent modifies one's external worldview to fit into the already existing cogitative structure or understanding of the person or subject) and *accommodation* (whereby the adolescent modifies one's cognitive schema or pattern of thinking to conform with new information concerning the external world); thus, the young person must make an adaptation that must include and adjust to new information (Lerner, pp. 90-91).

On an emotional level, a middle adolescent's personality may begin to change from the mild-mannered child to the irritated and moody teenager, which tends to resonate with the verisimilitude of adolescent lore. Adolescents are emerging as their own individuals, involving a differentiation of feelings, thoughts, judgments, and behaviors from that of their parents (Rice and Dolgin, p. 26). Anna Freud (1895-1982), Sigmund Freud's daughter, further amplified his theories that emotionally teenagers are plagued with these juxtaposed characteristics:

> ... internal conflict, psychic disequilibrium, and erratic behavior. Adolescents are on the one hand, egoistic, regarding themselves as the sole object of interest and the center of the universe, but on the other hand, also capable of self-sacrifice and devotion. They form passionate love relations, only to break them off suddenly. They sometimes desire complete social involvement and group participation and at other times solitude. They oscillate between blind submission to and rebellion against authority. They are selfish and material minded, but also full of lofty idealism. They are ascetic yet indulgent, inconsiderate of others yet touchy themselves. They swing between optimism and pessimism, between indefatigable enthusiasm and sluggishness and apathy. (1946, 159)

Consequently, the emotional behavior of adolescents will apparently have its eruptions as well as its soothing manifestations.

### 3. Late Adolescence

The last period or final stage of adolescent development is known as *late adolescence* and is generally correlated with post-secondary education (Shelton, p. 3). Characteristically, late adolescence encompasses the years from age 19 to 22, and usually involves life choices such as undergraduate studies, career decisions such as entering the workforce or military services, and possibly marriage. Late adolescents are now considered young adults by society because their issues are vastly different from that of a typical high school student, focusing on responsibilities that prepare them for life's challenges and entrance into adulthood. Although full adulthood usually means financial and economic independence apart from parental involvement, thus for many the period of adolescence can extend well beyond the age of twenty-two.

On a physical level, there is not much difference between middle adolescence and late adolescence beyond further development of muscular strength, size, and endurance. For young adult males there is rapid growth of auxiliary hair; a final change of voice deepening; growth of beard; and indentation of frontal hairline (Rice and Dolgin, 90). For young adult females there is growth of auxiliary hair; filling out of breasts to form adult conformation, and secondary breast development, that is, larger, rounder, firmer breasts with the areola receding and becoming incorporated into the breast itself so that only the nipple protrudes (Rice and Dolgin, pp. 90, 92).

On an intellectual level, during late adolescence there is a direct correlation between achieving high school success and going to college as distinct from going to a trade school or joining the workforce (Rice and Dolgin, p. 389). Therefore, mental ability is a determining factor in long-term vocational decisions. However, intelligence can also be measured by personal aspiration; young people who aspire to higher occupational choices demonstrate a higher propensity of academic ability.

On an emotional level, young people in their late teens and early twenties are full of promise and vulnerability, cynicism and faith, and ambiguity and achievement. According to educator and young adult expert Sharon Daloz Parks (2000), the reason for this dualism occurring in young adulthood is that for the first time they are experiencing "the birth of critical awareness and the dissolution and re-composition of the meaning of self, other, world, and 'God '"(p. 5). Late adolescence in young adults must provide meaning in their lives, and this emerging understanding affects college-age people in three areas: (1) becoming critically aware of their personal composing of reality; (2) self-consciously participating in an ongoing dialogue toward truth; and (3) cultivating a capacity to respond-acting-in ways that are satisfying and just (Daloz Parks, p. 6). Older adolescent emotions are also connected with religious expression.

In addition, there are social and cultural contextual changes occurring in adolescence: for younger adolescents, there is usually a change in school settings, transitioning from elementary school to junior high or middle school; similarly, during middle adolescent years, teenagers shift from junior high to high school, a transition that can be overwhelming and confusing; and in late adolescence there is the transition from high school to college, trade school, military, or the workforce. Indeed, adolescence can be a confusing and complex time in a person's life; therefore, it is critical that youth ministers learn the proper pastoral skills in nurturing young people as well as in enhancing their experience developmentally, to cope with the multiple transitions taking place in a short period of time. Therefore, it is critical that youth and campus ministers comprehend as much information as possible about adolescent development to increase their overall knowledge about adolescent behavior.

## Adolescent Development[4]

As established above, adolescent development is a unique period of transition from childhood to adulthood that spans a decade or more. Developmental psychologist Richard M. Lerner (2002) indicates that adolescence is a pronounced period of transition and stereotypes:

> Because of the dramatic and major ways in which change occurs in this period of life, the developmental tasks of adolescence can be especially problematic . . . adolescent changes can often appear more disruptive and disturbing in their effects on the individual and his or her social world than is the case with changes occurring in other periods of life. (p. 15)

This dramatic period of alteration causes over-generalized beliefs either misperceived by parents and adults or misperceived by teenagers and adults themselves. These exceptional simplifications are commonly known as stereotypes. This is the reason that some psychologists refer to the demanding time of pubescent evolution as "storm and stress."

## Adolescent Storm and Stress

The core belief concerning adolescent "storm and stress" is that the adolescent period of life is difficult and demanding not only for the adolescent, but for those around the adolescent as well. According to adolescent psychologist Jeffrey Jensen Arnett (2002), the stage of adolescent storm and stress involves three crucial elements:

> 1. **Conflict with parents.** Adolescents have a tendency to be rebellious and resist adult authority. In particular, adolescence is a time when conflict with parents is especially high.

> 2. **Mood disruptions.** Adolescents tend to be more volatile emotionally than either children or adults. They experience more extremes of mood, and more swings of mood from one extreme to the other. They also experience more frequent episodes of depressed mood than children or adults.

3. ***Risk behavior.*** Adolescents have a higher rate of reckless, norm-breaking, and antisocial behavior than either children or adults. Adolescents are more likely to cause disruption of social order, and to engage in behavior that carries the potential for harm to themselves and/or the people around them. (pp. 8-9)

These three elements characterize the period of storm and stress; however, the above three issues that clarify adolescent conduct are certainly not an exhaustive list.

Interestingly, the three different elements of storm and stress correlate with the three different periods of adolescence (early, middle, late) and each element (conflict, mood, risk) within each period has its own unique difficulty. Conflict with parents peaks with early adolescent ages 11-14, mood disruptions is heightened in middle adolescent ages 15-18, and risk behavior climaxes in late adolescent ages 19-22 (Arnett, p. 9). The main reason for the correlation between the three elements and the three periods of adolescence is that each element presents diverse types of complexities to be experienced, for both adolescents and their surrounding adults.

Developmental psychologists have debated storm and stress for more than fifty years (Lerner, p. 17). Current research regarding adolescent storm and stress indicates that the overwhelming majority of adolescents in the United States do not experience a "stormy" or "stressful" adolescence. Albeit, there might be a few "bumps in the road," most young people adopt the same set of values, beliefs, and standards set by their parents and form friendships with similar-minded peers (Lerner, p. 18). According to Arnett (2002), "Currently, there is evidence that adolescent storm and stress may be more likely in the majority culture-the largely White middle class-than in other cultures that are part of [North] American society" (p. 13). For Arnett, adolescent storm and stress is no myth to capture popular imagination, or some psychological construct conceived by developmental psychologists to sell books, but is a genuine part of adolescent life. The awesome challenge for those working with teenagers is to help them to make a paradox out of adolescent life in becoming not only a period of storm and stress, but a period of exuberant joy and energetic growth.

The phase of storm and stress can also be related to physical and cognitive changes that are taking place in the lives of adolescents. Biological changes and cogitative changes may be heightened because storm and stress may be a combination of various changing areas with a young person's life. Arnett notes that, "A substantial amount of adolescent storm and stress arises from regulating the pace of adolescents' growing independence" (p. 13). Since rapid independence is occurring during adolescence-biological, intellectual, and sexual-these swift changes may create storm and stress among certain teenage individuals.

Consequently, it may be useful for youth ministers to address the phase of adolescent storm and stress with parents and adult volunteer leaders within the youth ministry. Youth ministers may want to conduct catechetical sessions with parents who would present and discern current research regarding U.S. teenage behavior.

## Adolescent Identity

Most youth living in the United States of America live good, healthy, and well-adjusted lives. Average U.S. teenagers grow up in supportive families, have friends, attend good schools, engage in sports, have artistic interests, have part-time jobs, date a little, or even have a serious boyfriend or girlfriend (Lerner, p. 140). Therefore, life for the average teenager in the United States is pretty good! However, for many, life is less than ideal and some youth come from highly dysfunctional families, live in poverty, and attend run-down, decaying schools. The neighborhoods of many inner-cities are often in rapid decline. Consequently, local role models are often delinquents, criminals, and "gangsters," who teach vulnerable adolescents about stealing, drug dealing, and prostitution. Therefore, emphasizing adolescent identity formation is significant because it is this feature of the individual young person that directly results from past and present encounters, and contributes to future outcomes. Teenage life often involves two key aspects: (1) finding something to do and (2) finding someone to be, both catapult the adolescents in search of personal expression and identity choices.

## Adolescent Culture

Below are poignant words from sociologist Christian Smith (Smith and Denton 2005) that introduced the National Study of Youth and Religion, which was conducted from July 2002 to April 2003, had surveyed 3,370 adolescents, and was written and published in useable fashion as *Soul Searching: The Religious and Spiritual Lives of American Teenagers.*

> American teenagers can embody adults' highest hopes and most gripping fears. They represent a radiant energy that opens doors to the future for families, communities, and society. But they also evoke deep adult anxieties about teen rebellion, trouble, and broken and compromised lives. Parents, teachers, and youth workers behold their teenagers with pride, hope, and enjoyment, but also often worry, distress, and frustration. How are our teenagers doing in life? What is happening to our relationships with them? How will they turn out? Happy and responsible? Troubled and depressed? Or worse? Such personal ambivalent feelings about teenagers are amplified in the discourse and images that animate our culture and institutions. Our youth, it is often said, are the future, our hope for a brighter world. Teenagers are exciting, zany, inventive, fun. We adults love them dearly, we tell ourselves, and would do anything to make their lives happy and full. And yet, adults see and fear in adolescence a dark side as well. Surly indifference and defiance.

> Dangerous peer pressure. Parties. Foolish choices. Drugs. Drunk driving. Crime. Pregnancy. Abortions. AIDS. Suspensions. School dropouts. School shootings. Suicide. So, many adults worry deeply that, whatever good there is, something may also be profoundly wrong about the lives of American teenagers. (p. 3)

American youth comprise a myriad of complexities that deserve attention and compose a certain slice of the American population that has great influence.

Adolescent culture is significant and can be categorized as a subculture, which suggests that adolescents are uniform peer group whose values might be different from, and contrary to, adult values. The adolescent subculture exists predominantly in high school, where the high school constitutes a small-governed society and one that has little interaction with the outside adult society. High schools, by their nature, are designed to be segregated to some extent from the outside world and thus develop a subculture distinct from adult culture.

It does not take long to recognize that United States teenagers have their own image, language, styles, and interests that typically differ from their parents, especially if parents do not present a unified front (Rice and Dolgin, p. 310). Tension may exist between parents and adolescents because society is gearing adolescents to exercise a certain amount of autonomy and to make their own decisions because, for the majority, after high school life comes to a close, college life begins, and a certain amount of self-control and self-direction is needed in order to survive. Tensions also occur in teenagers because they are experiencing both identity formation issues and cognitive changes, and both can cause stress, anxiety, and tension. Nevertheless, there are notable disagreements between adults and adolescents while they co-exist with one another under the same roof: slang-language, styles of dress, tastes in music, preferences of popular movies, dating customs, and places where youth hang-out, to name a few. Thus peer associations will sometimes be counter to adult preferences (Rice and Dolgin, p. 311). The major reason for the disagreements between teenagers and their parents is the disparity between youthful behavior and adult values. Young people are still in process, and therefore, their life styles and behavior are in process as well. There are two significant areas in which adolescents and adults seem to disagree more than any other single issue: (1) sexual attitudes and behavior, which tend in adolescents to be more liberal than those of their parents and (2) drugs and drug use, which reflect the attitude "if they are not bothering anyone, let them use drugs" (Rice and Dolgin, p. 312). Regarding sexual behavior, the majority of young people who are openly admitting to having sex do not maintain the position that oral sex is tantamount to sexual intercourse, despite adult beliefs.

In one study of fundamentalist, Bible-based Christian adolescents, youth were compared to mainline American youth, which demonstrated that Christian principles can determine life style and can influence adolescent culture.[5] Three areas were studied; they represent areas in which adolescents and adults have tensions: alcohol use, drug use, and pre-marital sex. The study was conducted among teenage 12th graders (see Strommen and Hardel, 2000; p. 264).

| Item | Christian Youth | American Youth |
|---|---|---|
| Alcohol use six or more times in one year. | 15% | 54% |
| Marijuana use one or more times in the last year. | 11% | 20% |
| Sexual intercourse one or more times in your lifetime. | 27% | 63% |

Although the statistics are not particularly shocking, they do represent areas that need further catechesis both inside and outside the Sunday pulpit. These are all indicators that suggest that adolescent culture is different from adult culture-or is it?

Sociologist Robert N. Bellah (1985) suggests that adolescent culture mirrors adult culture; that is, every person is a byproduct of their cultural milieu. Bellah's research concluded that American culture was influenced by people's moral, religious, and intellectual dispositions-their internal views, outlooks, and ideas that shaped people's conceptual and contextual framework (p. 82). Bellah refers to this cultural and individual enterprise as "habits of the heart." Bellah notes that one of the guiding principles that dictate personal and collective habits of the heart is individualism. American culture assumes that the meaning and purpose in life is becoming an individual and autonomous. This mindset, of course, has its limitations and some subsequent patterns prevalent in society today are low commitment to work productivity, high divorce rate, and a low attendance at Sunday services. Therefore, it is safe to speculate that "habits of the heart" for American teenagers begin well before adolescence.

Theologian Henry Richard Niebuhr (1951) in his classic exposition, *Christ and Culture*, argues for five stances or approaches that Christians have related with culture over time that can be applicable to U.S. youth culture today: (1) Christ against culture, a separation from the world; (2) Christ of culture, an accommodation to culture; (3) Christ above culture, a synthesis of Christ and culture; (4) Christ and culture in paradox, a theology of dualism; and (5) Christ, the transformer of culture, a conversion of culture (xliii-lx). It is Niebuh's fifth stance that youth ministers may want to read and carry forth as a positive theological and pastoral position.

One of the largest areas of concern in adolescent culture is materialism. Clothing, cars, computers, video games, and cellular phones all represent symbols of materialism for adolescents. From a purely sociological standpoint, American teenagers have immense purchasing power, which makes them a prime target for advertising agencies, according to Christian Smith (2005):

> Industry experts estimate that American teenagers spend about $170 billion of their own dollars annually and influence upwards of *$500 billion* of their parents ' spending. American teenagers thus have an immense amount of money to spend in the market. In addition, they are both highly brand-sensitive and brand-flexible. This means that, while they will spend extra money to purchase a particular product brand that is in fashion, their brand preferences are often not firmly established. (p.178)

These statistics are staggering, but they reflect that capitalistic consumerism exists not only with American adults, but with adolescents as well.

There are further statistics that help make ministry more difficult for youth pastors. Although cellular phone use is the highest it has ever been in this country among young people (because it represents cutting-edge technology), many youth spend a great deal of time using alternative forms of communication via their personal computers. Approximately 41 percent of American 18-to-24 year-olds report using online chat rooms to communicate with peers, many of them daily or weekly; this rate is the highest of any age group; and likewise, more than 60 percent use e-mail (Rice and Dolgin, 323). The average adolescent watches 21 hours of television per week and views 360,000 television advertisements before graduating from high school. These statistics reinforce the earlier statement that advertisement companies recognize that as a subculture, adolescents are a force to be reckoned with (Smith, 179). Moreover, 65 percent of 8-to-18-year-olds have their own television set in their bedrooms (Smith, 179). American adolescent culture has come about not by accident; it is a $240-billion-per-year advertising industry that purposely targets youth and sometimes causes the worst human potentials to surface within American teenagers: vanity, envy, jealousy, pride, insecurity, impulsiveness, and sexual obsessiveness.

Like all things in life, time has a way of fading out trends and memories. Below is a chart that highlights changes in tastes of fashion, music, and cinema (adapted and modified from Rice and Dolgin, p. 324).

The table on pg. 44 demonstrates that adolescent tastes change over the years and there is no reason to suggest that today 's adolescents will not be experiencing the same tensions with their teenagers once they, too, become functioning adults and parents in society.

The task to reverse this reality is vast and seemingly irreversible, but those who minister to adolescents need not give up hope. The path that youth ministers take with their young people to offset these consumer and materialistic trends-which are occurring at such a high rate of speed in the lives of teenagers-will only naturally influence and determine the character and integrity of American adolescents; in other words, youth ministers would be wise to foster a deeper Catholic worldview in Catholic adolescents to help offset the worldly trends. Gospel values, ethics, morality, virtuous living, sacraments, frugality, discipleship, and stewardship deserve to be presented to Catholic young people as a way to safeguard against consumer and materialistic tends. Moreover, these trends will loom large on adolescent culture and faith, and especially adolescent conversion and spirituality if Catholic ideals and principles are *not* instilled and fostered in teenagers by well informed Catholic youth ministers.

## Adolescent Conversion

One of the principal aims of youth ministry is to facilitate the adolescent along the journey of conversion. The years of adolescence are ripe for religious conversion and transformation. There are religious organizations, church-specific youth ministries, and para-church agencies that all help adolescent conversion take place within the life of a teenager. As *Renewing the Vision: A Framework for Catholic Youth Ministry* (1997) explains, the goal of conversion is "to foster the total personal and spiritual growth of each young person" (15). Therefore, RTV

| Decade | Clothing | Cinema | Music |
|---|---|---|---|
| 1950s | Rolled jeans, white t-shirt, saddle shoes, sweater sets | *From Here to Eternity* and 3-D horror films | Elvis Presley, Buddy Holly, Little Richard, Chuck Berry, Bill Haley and the Comets |
| 1960s | Torn jeans, headbands, Afros, granny glasses, tie-dyed T-shirts | *Lawrence of Arabia; To Kill a Mockingbird;* Alfred Hitchcock | The Beatles, the Beach Boys, Bob Dylan, the Grateful Dead, Jimi Hendrix, Janice Joplin |
| 1970s | Bell-bottoms, Earth shoes, crocheted vests, disco styles | *American Graffiti; Star Wars; Jaws* | The Eagles; Led Zepplin; Fleetwood Mac; America; Pink Floyd, Crosby, Stills, Nash, & Young |
| 1980s | Acid-washed jeans, leg warmers, leggings, "big hair," and mullet cuts | *Raiders of the Lost Ark; Top Gun; Back to the Future* | Michael Jackson; U2; Genesis; Journey; the Pretenders; Talking Heads; Metallica |
| 1990s | Baggy pants, tattoos, piercings, fleece, grunge-look | *Jurassic Park; The Matrix; Star Wars: Prequel Series* | Nirvana; Pearl Jam; Sonic Youth; Nine-Inch Nails; Phish; Hootie and the Blowfish; Dave Matthews Band |
| 2000s | Low-cut jeans, fitted T-shirts, button-front shirts, straight hair | *Lord of the Rings trilogy; American Pie; Harry Potter* | Creed; Matchbox Twenty; Cheryl Crow, Brittney Spears; Christiana Aguilera; Jessica Simpson |
| 2010s | Boots, suede belts, dark denim hipsters, updated gypsy look | *Avatar; Clash of the Titans; Transformers, Iron Man* | Miley Cyrus Jonas Brothers; Taylor Swift; Amy Lee |

recognizes the importance of adolescent conversion with the life of teenagers and within the context of youth ministry. Likewise, the *General Directory for Catechesis* (1997) also maintains that conversion is a primary component for quality parish-based and campus-based ministries: "it [conversion] is at the heart of faith and arises from the depth of the human person" (n. 55). Similar to RTV, the GDC also acknowledges the significance of conversion within each person. Unfortunately, according to Canales (2005b), "not all Catholic youth ministries or ministers focus on conversion. Some youth ministers do not want to get too 'religious' with teenagers. This is an enormous mistake because many youth yearn for spiritual renewal and crave deeper theological insight" (44). From a theological and pastoral perspective, adolescent conversion is a topic or theme that merits serious attention within comprehensive youth ministry.

## Summary

The importance of this discussion on adolescence is the wide range of adolescent topics and this chapter only scratches the surface. I have only vaguely addressed topics such as the periods of adolescence and adolescent developmental theories (identity formation), but did not touch upon cognitive, moral, faith developmental theories. The importance of understanding adolescent psychological issues for youth ministry is crucial for the ministry to stand by, with, and for young people. Teenagers are God's gift, loved and appreciated for who they are, and are powerfully important to the life of the Church and society. Consequently, it is the role and responsibility of the local community, parents, and youth minister to ensure that young people do not become unnoticed, but are empowered to become healthy, thriving, and productive members of the church today, not only in the future when they start earning a permanent income, but today-now and immediately.

## Discussion Questions

(1) Explain the relationship that youth ministry and adolescent psychology have together. Do you see the relevance and connection between them?

(2) Discuss the period of "storm and stress" within adolescent life. Can you pinpoint any such behavior in your own journey through the adolescent years?

(3) Why is it important for adult youth leaders/catechists and youth ministers to become familiar with the period of adolescence?

(4) Review the adolescent culture section areas outlined above and discuss its significance for you. Explain your rationale.

(5) Name some of the ways that you can integrate this material and develop it into comprehensive Catholic youth ministry settings, events, and programs.

## CHAPTER TWO

# DEFINING, DESCRIBING, AND SITUATING CATHOLIC ADOLESCENT SPIRITUALITY

*"Youth ministry is TO youth when the Christian community exercises its pastoral role in meeting young people's needs. Youth ministry is WITH youth because young people share with adults a common responsibility to carry out the Church's mission. Youth ministry is BY youth when young people exercise their own ministry to others, particularly to their peers. Youth ministry is FOR youth in that adult youth ministers attempt to interpret the needs of youth and act as advocates in articulating youth's legitimate concerns to the wider community."*[6]

**A Vision of Youth Ministry**
*1976, Department of [Catholic] Education; USCC*

Cultivating Christian spirituality in Catholic adolescents is not a new idea. It has been a process that parents, youth ministers, and pastors have been trying to capture and instill in young people for generations. As remarkable as it might seem, a dearth of adolescent resources have been published over the years to discuss teenage spirituality in particular. Adolescent spirituality, in Catholic circles, is usually glossed-over or lumped together with other Christian ministry categories such as catechesis, discipleship, or evangelization. However, in recent years there has been a resurgence of teenage spirituality around the world (Mehlman, 2000; Wright, 2000; Abbott-Chapman & Denholm, 2001; Crawford & Rossiter, 2004; Engebretson, 2004, 2006; McQuillan 2004; Tacey, 2004; Baker, 2005; White, 2005, 2008; Yaconelli, 2005, 2006; Canales, 2005, 2006, 2007; Pupura, 2008).

Moreover, it is important to note that the reflections in this chapter are limited to a religious context and specifically a Christian context, and even more particularly with Catholic American teenagers' quest for spirituality. Consequently, this chapter will not consider the spirituality of adolescents from other faith traditions or world religions despite their sacred relevance and/or the depth of their piety.

Furthermore, this author is well aware of Catholic sociologist's David J. Tacey's (2004) findings on the emergence of contemporary spirituality in youth or as he has coined it-"the spirituality revolution"-an all-inclusive, secular, broad, democratic, and non-hierarchical model of spirituality (pp. 30-46). Although this author does not disagree with Tacey's assessment, this chapter will not explore the spirituality in this new context as a form of personal religion that cultivates Catholic adolescent spirituality.

This chapter has two goals in mind: (1) to offer a brief description of Christian teenage spirituality and (2) to situate adolescent spirituality in the context of comprehensive Catholic youth ministry. While much more work needs to be done to fully understand adolescent spirituality and the process of which to cultivate and awaken spirituality in American Catholic teenagers, a helpful beginning will be to define spirituality and identify its proper place in Catholic youth ministry.

## Defining and Describing Adolescent Spirituality

Christian spirituality is concerned with an individual's personal and communal response to God and growth in Jesus Christ. Adolescent spirituality is a "slice" of Christian spirituality that directly caters to the intellectual, emotional, pastoral, and spiritual needs of young people. A variety of definitions for adolescent spirituality are offered in this section to illustrate the spectrum of reality behind the phenomena of interpreting the presence of God.

Andrew Wright (2000) states, "spirituality is a notoriously difficult term to define . . . at the heart of spirituality is that which is both mysterious and dynamic" (p. 7). Adolescent spirituality is elusive and vibrant, and is caught in a healthy tension between the sacred and profane (Wright, 2000; McQuillan, 2004; Tacey, 2004).

Catholic religious educator Kathleen Engebretson (2006) describes adolescent spirituality as having four components.

> [Adolescent] spirituality is: (1) experience of the sacred other which is accompanied by feelings of wonder, joy, love, trust, and hope; (2) connectedness with responsibility for the self, other people, and the non-human world; (3) the illumination of lived experience with meaning and value; (4) the need for name and expression in either traditional or non-traditional ways. (p. 330)

Even in the narrow discussion of Catholic teenage spirituality the definition is multifaceted and sophisticated. However, it is Engebretson's (2006) first component that is most beneficial to this essay because adolescents cannot find words to talk about God until they have had an *experience* of God about which to talk (p. 331).

Catholic educator, Jane C. Lindle (2005), observes, "[Adolescent] spirituality is multidimensional and includes an individual relationship with God, as well as a communal relationship with God and other people" (p. 11). Conversely, adolescent spirituality requires personal awareness and connection with the community. For Lindle (2005), another component of adolescent spirituality is service, "The development of a young person's spirituality requires opportunities for service . . . and making service-learning a constant part of catechesis and youth activities" (pp. 9, 33). Service can be a rewarding ministry for all young people and will definitely enhance personal and communal spirituality.

Mark Yaconelli has written about adolescent spirituality in his two volumes: *Growing Souls: Experiments in Contemplative Youth Ministry* (2005) *and Contemplative Youth Ministry: Practicing the Presence of Jesus* (2006).[7] Yoconelli (2005) defines youth spirituality this way, "Spirituality seeks to remind us of the nearness of God, our relatedness to Christ, and the inspiration (in-Spiriting) of the Holy Spirit-all of which empower us for acts of mercy, justice, and peace in the world" (p. 280). For Yaconelli, teenage spirituality is connected to one's experience with God and leads to action and service. Spirituality is not focused on tenets of the faith (doctrines, creeds), apologetics (defending one's faith), morality (behavior, sexuality), or emotionality (praise music, charismatic phenomenon), but is motivated by an earnest desire to encounter the triune God and to recover the universal call to holiness (Yaconelli, 2005, p. 280).

Catholic religious educators Marisa Crawford and Graham Rossiter (1996) note that youth have a more secularized spirituality that is intertwined with religious practices. They state,

> Youth in industrialized, urbanized societies see people negotiating life and forming values more from their own initiative, with less dependence on traditional religious guidance. For those [young people], religion no longer speaks with relevance or authority; if they have concerns about the environment, human rights, personal relationships, and sexuality, they are more likely to refer to organizations in society which are unaffiliated

> with religion. In their self-understanding and self-expression many youth are eclectic, drawing on elements in trans-cultural, trans-ethnic, and trans-religious ways-the mass media, especially [Internet], television, film, and music are significant sources. (p. 133)

All this alternative secular stimulation helps to form and influence teenagers to think and respond in diverse ways to the efforts of youth ministers who are trying to pass on the Catholic faith, religious traditions, Christian identity, and spirituality. Hence, some adolescents might operate out of a secular spirituality that is infused with a youth spirituality that concentrates on Christian values and ideals.

Catholic theologian Sharon Reed (1991a) suggests that a vision for developing youth spirituality is twofold: (1) there must be an awareness of who and what I am called to be and (2) an awareness that demands response-one nourishes the other (p. 4). These are the classical existential questions: Who am I? Why am I here? Where do I fit in? What will I do with my life? Therefore, adolescence is a ripe time for spiritual growth and formation.

Catholic Archbishop Emeritus of Cincinnati, Ohio, Daniel E. Pilarczyk (1986) defines adolescent spirituality in three ways:

> (1) Spirituality is not a matter of acquiring something new. Youth already have spirituality by virtue of faith and baptism; it is simply a matter of being consistent with God.

> (2) Spirituality is the gift of holiness, a gift that God bestows on all people, but youth need to be willing and open to respond to the gift of holiness.

> (3) Spirituality is living in the Lord, which is a direct response and acceptance to the call of holi-

ness and brings Christ out of the shadows of our lives to the forefront of our existence (pp. 2-3).

Recognizing these three dimensions will assist Catholic youth ministers in helping to readily identify spirituality in adolescents' lives.

Psychologist and Jesuit priest Charles M. Shelton (1983), in one of the first Catholic books dealing with this subject, *Adolescent Spirituality: Pastoral Ministry for High School and College Youth*, notes that there are four key characteristics of adolescent spirituality. For Shelton, adolescent Christian spirituality should be: (1) Christ-centered, (2) relational, (3) future-oriented, and (4) developmental (pp. 9-10). It is meritorious to discuss each characteristic briefly because Shelton's work is highly regarded in Catholic adolescent circles and is used as a reference point by many Catholic scholars, and its wide usage has established it as a fundamental text in the area of adolescent spirituality.

*Christ-centered*: For Shelton, adolescent spirituality "focuses on the personal, loving invitation given the adolescent to 'come, follow me'-to walk the path of Jesus, while increasingly realizing what journeying with Jesus really means" (p. 9). Developing and sustaining the personal relationship between teenager and Christ is absolutely necessary to cultivating and maintaining spiritual awareness in adolescents. Introducing teenagers to Christ, building meaningful relationships with Christ, and sustaining those relationships to Christ are at the very heart of comprehensive youth ministry and Christian discipleship.

*Relational*: Youth ministry is a highly relational ministry. Shelton notes, "Human relationships also enter the adolescent's experience for spiritual growth, and this growth is concerned with ultimate meanings and values, but it is incarnated in human encounters and circumstances" (p. 9). A teenager's experience of relationships with family, friends, and significant adults within the community impacts a young person's spiritual worldview. This author, Canales (2006), observed in an earlier academic article that healthy friendships in youth ministry revolve around three fronts: "(a) teaching that Jesus is a friend of teenagers, (b) establishing healthy friendships between adults and adolescents, and (c) creating an atmosphere for fostering friendships among youth" (p. 208). Examining the various friendships and relationships that young people encounter helps them to grow in self-identity and spiritual awareness.

*Future-oriented:* Adolescents are continually adopting ideas, concepts, values, and strategies for future-orientated living. Shelton maintains that teenagers often understand spirituality as something that happens to them in the future.

> Developmentally the adolescent grows more outward. Even though the future is by no means secure, adolescents are willing to explore and to attempt answers to life's questions. The adolescent begins to forge a mature identity that is made personally meaningful in the context of his or her current developmental level. Adolescent spirituality speaks to this present life in the context of the adolescent's future growth possibilities. (p. 10)…

In order to cultivate spiritual awareness in adolescents, youth ministers need not only to encourage the immediate and present spiritual condition of teenagers, but also to encourage the future potentiality, the not-yet or yet-to-be future spiritual situation of young people.

*Developmental:* From a developmental perspective, teenagers go through an assortment of changes: physical, intellectual, emotional, sexual, and spiritual. Shelton reports, "Spirituality for adolescents needs to make use of these developmental insights in order to enhance the adult's understanding of the adolescent's understanding of his or her own spiritual growth" (p. 10). Cultivating adolescent spirituality requires that youth ministers empower teenagers to encounter all aspects of life: social and spiritual as well as the sacred and the profane. Sharon Reed (1991b) states that spirituality for young people should include developmental insights and perspectives.

"Adolescents must be given *all the time they need* to come to an understanding of the scope of their spirituality. We adults also need to understand this developmental stage if we are to be fully present to all the dynamics as they unfold" (p. 96).

Cultivating teenage spirituality requires that adults have an appreciation for adolescent developmental perspectives and awareness that young people will grow in holiness and dedicate themselves to God in different ways and at different times. These four key characteristics of adolescent spirituality help maturing adolescents become more spiritually attuned as they walk the journey of conversion, faith, and Christian commitment (Shelton, p. 338). The theoretical grounding in Shelton's work is still solid, applicable, and appropriate after these many years, and today's youth ministers can garner much from his research.

The authors mentioned offer their own critical insights to help to define adolescent spirituality and provide a pivotal backdrop for the connectedness between juveniles and youth ministry. Although fostering adolescent spirituality may seem like a foregone conclusion on the part of parish youth ministers, some of the methods for trying to attain a more mature spirituality may be challenging for young people, but the majority are youth-friendly and are time-tested and true, especially if they are properly facilitated by an experienced youth minister and situated in the context of comprehensive Catholic youth ministry.

## Situating Adolescent Spirituality in the Context of Comprehensive Catholic Youth Ministry

Adolescent spirituality is an undergirding element of Catholic comprehensive youth ministry as defined in the official U.S. Catholic documents *A Vision of Youth Ministry* (1976) and *Renewing the Vision: A Framework for Catholic Youth Ministry* (1997). In the updated *Renewing the Vision* (1997, henceforth RTV) the U.S. Catholic Bishops state that there are three goals of comprehensive Catholic youth ministry: :

> **Goal 1**: To *empower* young people to live as disciples of Jesus Christ in our world today (p. 9)
>
> **Goal 2**: To *draw* young people to responsible participation in the life, mission, and work of the Catholic faith community (p. 11)
>
> **Goal 3**: To *foster* the total person and spiritual growth of each young person (p. 15)

The three goals of RTV are like pillars that support the Catholic youth ministry infrastructure. For Catholics engaging in juvenile ministry in the United States, these goals are an ecclesial mandate, which Catholic youth ministers and pastors must utilize as guidelines that promote spiritually healthy ministry to adolescents. Goal 2 highlights the communal dimension of cultivating adolescent spirituality and Catholic teenage spiritual formation. Regarding Goal 2, RTV states,

> Young people experience the Catholic community of faith at home, in the parish (especially in youth ministry programs), in Catholic schools, and in other organizations serving youth. Ministry with adolescents recognizes the importance of each of these faith communities in helping young people grow in faith as they experience life in community and actively participate in the mission of Jesus Christ and his Church. (p. 11)

Goal 3 is most relevant to our understanding of the place of adolescent spirituality in youth ministry. Regarding Goal 3, RTV states,

> Ministry with adolescents promotes the growth of healthy, competent, caring, and faith-filled Catholic young people. The Church is concerned for the whole person, addressing the young

person's spiritual needs in the context of his or her whole life. Ministry with adolescents fosters positive adolescent development and growth in both Christian discipleship and Catholic identity. Promoting the [spiritual] growth of young and older adolescents means addressing their unique developmental, social, and religious needs and nurturing the qualities or assets necessary for positive development. It also means addressing the objective obstacles to healthy growth that affect the lives of so many young people, such as poverty, racial discrimination, and social injustice, as well as the subjective obstacles to healthy growth such as the loss of a sense of sin, the influence of values promoted by the secular media, and the negative impact of the consumer mentality. (p. 15)

Cultivating adolescent spirituality is of major interest to the U.S. Catholic Bishops and Goals 2 and 3 of RTV emphasize that point. In addition, teaching and developing a sense of the sacred within teenagers is the responsibility of the entire church and is part of comprehensive youth ministry (RTV, p. 11).

The term "comprehensive" is extremely important for Catholic youth ministry in the United States because it describes the systematic and integrated approach to youth ministry outlined in *Renewing the Vision* and is the preferred approach to ministry with adolescents (Canales, 2007, p. 59). Comprehensive youth ministry stresses the moral, spiritual, and faith development of adolescents while incorporating young people into the mission and ministry of Jesus Christ. Furthermore, comprehensive youth ministry concentrates on the universal church and local church or diocese (there are approximately 195 Catholic dioceses in the United States), and not merely on the parochial church or parish (equivalent to Protestant congregation), although this is where the majority of youth ministry happens.

> Comprehensive Catholic youth ministry means that youth ministers and adolescents alike become increasingly aware that the Catholic faith is for them-all of it-not only selective parts. That is to suggest, ministry to adolescents ideally moves beyond a ministry that focuses on "my youth group" or "my parish" to embrace a larger ecclesiastical worldview: universal church, preferential option for the poor, family, multiculturalism, intergenerational, diocese, etc. (Canales, 2007, p. 60)

Therefore, comprehensive Catholic youth ministry situates ministry to adolescents in a larger pastoral framework and context beyond the boundaries of a particular congregation.

The U.S. Conference of Catholic Bishops (1997) offers a set of guidelines and working definitions for youth ministers and youth catechists to follow while doing comprehensive youth ministry.

The comprehensive framework for ministry with adolescents is designed to:

> 1. Utilize each of the Church's ministries-advocacy, catechesis, community life, evangelization, justice and service, leadership development, pastoral care, prayer and worship-in an integrated approach to achieving the three goals for ministry with adolescents.
>
> 2. Provide developmentally appropriate programs and activities that promote personal and spiritual growth for young and older adolescents.
>
> 3. Enrich family life and promote the faith growth of families of adolescents.

4. Incorporate young people fully into all aspects of church life and engage them in ministry and leadership in the faith community.

5. Create partnerships among families, schools, churches, and community organizations in a common effort to promote positive youth development (RTV, 20).

The guidelines for comprehensive youth ministry are an important dimension for Catholic youth ministry and are crucial for helping youth ministers in their quest to cultivate adolescent spirituality.

Cultivating adolescent spirituality is closely aligned with the eighth component in RTV, prayer and worship. Concerning prayer and worship, RTV reads,

> The ministry of prayer and worship *celebrates* and *deepens* young people's relationship with Jesus Christ through the bestowal of grace, communal prayer and liturgical experiences; it *awakens* their awareness of the [Holy] Spirit at work in their lives; it *incorporates* young people more fully into the sacramental life of the Church, especially [Sunday] Eucharist; it *nurtures* the personal prayer life of young people; and it *fosters* family rituals and prayer. (RTV, 44)

Prayer and worship are essential for enhancing adolescent spirituality. The quest for adolescent spirituality takes place on many different levels and in diverse ministry settings.

In Kathleen Engebretson's (2004) survey of twenty teenage boys, ages 15 to 17 years, she observed that spirituality was expressed in the lives of the boys "in prayer and in personal and communal rituals" (p. 275). In Engebretson's investigation, "Most participants said that they prayed, but did not describe what their prayer was like . . . the frequency of prayer and the forms of prayer" (p. 275). Furthermore, "The majority expressed belief in God [and found] prayer is used to express spirituality" in Catholic adolescent boys (p. 276). The good news is Catholic adolescent males pray; the bad news is they do not pray in a systematic and intentional way as RTV describes.

According to Yaconelli (2005), strengthening spirituality in Catholic adolescents is important for comprehensive youth ministry for several reasons: (1) current approaches to youth ministry *neglect* the spiritual life of youth ministers, adult youth leaders (volunteers), parents of teenagers, and the youth themselves; (2) juvenile workers and youth *desire* to experience God within their own lives; (3) parishes of *transformed* adults, living lives of prayer and service, attract and help to change the hearts, minds, and lives of young people; and (4) youth *yearn* to recognize God's presence in their lives, discern God's will, and to be empowered to live out their vocation (pp. 27-34).

Therefore, one task of parish youth ministers is to provide quality approaches, opportunities, and creative moments for adults and teenagers to become more spiritually attuned to God. There are a multitude of methods that youth ministers can use to enhance an adolescent's spirituality; the pastoral imperative is finding the proper spiritual strategies that work for a specific group of adolescents doing a particular activity, trying to accomplish a precise result.

## Some Methods for Strengthening Catholic Adolescent Spirituality

Undoubtedly, there are numerous methods for trying to help Catholic adolescents develop a keener sense of spirituality (Canales, 2009a, pp. 11-18; Canales, 2009b, pp. 65-74). In this brief section, three areas are identified that address the progress of adolescent spirituality in Catholic circles. Three areas for cultivating adolescent spirituality are identified: (1) typical methods used by youth ministers, (2) U.S. Catholic Bishops' recommendations for enhancing adolescent spirituality, and (3) additional miscellaneous suggestions offered by other Catholic writers.

## 1. Typical Methods Used by Youth Ministers

Catholic youth ministers may decide to provide spiritual activities and catechetical formation that aid in cultivating the interior life of adolescents in order that they may encounter the various facets of God. Such spiritual activities and catechetical formation may correspond with the aforementioned adolescent spirituality characteristics that Shelton discusses. Youth ministers, adult youth leaders (volunteers), and parents would be wise to stimulate the sacred within the lives of young people and develop the characteristics found in adolescent spirituality. There are a myriad of ways to enhance adolescent spirituality. Here are three tried and true pastoral methods to enhance adolescent spirituality: "(1) creative prayer experiences, (2) inspirational worship, and (3) weekend retreats" (Canales, 2006, p. 210).

A great way to boost adolescent spirituality is through creative prayer experiences; the National Federation for Catholic Youth Ministry (1997) document titled *From Age to Age: The Challenge of Worship with Adolescents* observes that creative worship involves several areas: youth being involved in the life of the parish, youth feeling accepted and invited to participate in worship, fostering personal and communal prayer, effective preaching of the word of God, a youthful spirit, music, and song, and interactivity (pp. 43-52). Another way to enhance adolescent spirituality is by providing teenagers with inspirational worship, and in the Catholic tradition, and according to the Second Vatican Council (1963-1965), this implies engaging young people through full participation, active participation, and conscious participation in the sacred liturgy (*Sacrosanctum Concilium*, n. 14). Michael Warren (1991) — a pioneer in Catholic youth ministry studies — maintains that retreats are an excellent way to increase adolescent spirituality and have "made a remarkable contribution to the renewal of youth ministry" in the Catholic Church (pp. 5, 14). Taken together, these three areas will foster a deeper and more meaningful spirituality in the lives of adolescents.

## 2. The U.S. Catholic Bishops' Recommendations for Enhancing Adolescent Spirituality

Beyond RTV, creative prayer experiences, inspirational worship, and weekend retreats, the Catholic Church offers good recommendations for a systematic spiritual formation that caters to adolescents. In Catholic circles, cultivating adolescent spirituality is more than a haphazard use of various spiritual practices. The Catholic Church has some specific and deliberate guidelines for what a complete spiritual formation process might encompass in a diocese or parish for adolescents. The U.S. Catholic Bishops' (2005) statement on lay ministry, *Co-Workers in the Vineyard of the Lord*, offers ten elements of enhancing personal spiritual awareness: (1) living in union with Christ, (2) faith-formation built on the word of God, (3) spiritual foundation based on liturgy, especially the sacraments, (4) an incarnational outlook on life and a paschal theology of loving service, (5) an awareness of sin, (6) an understanding of suffering, (7) an appreciation and affection for Mary of Nazareth, (8) love for the Church, (9) devotion to the Eucharist, and (10) an ecumenical spirit (pp. 39-41). The document maintains that taken together, these ten elements afford a person a "school of holiness," which "promotes and strengthens that fundamental conversion that places God, and not oneself, at the center of one's life" (p. 38). Encouraging spirituality, self-awareness, and spiritual development is a complete process that encompasses many facets of the Christian life.

## 3. Additional Suggestions

Two spiritual writers: one a theologian, Richard P. McBrien and the other Bishop Emeritus, Daniel E. Pilarczyk offer additional suggestions to enhance spirituality in Catholic adults that can be integrated into the lives of Catholic teenagers. These additional areas can also be developed to increase adolescent spirituality and might include the fostering of the theological virtues of faith, hope, and love, which have God as their proper and immediate object and are described by the Apostle Paul in 1 Corinthians 13:13. In addition, stressing the cardinal virtues of prudence, justice, fortitude, and temperance may also increase personal spiritual awareness and character.

Catholic theologian Richard P. McBrien (1995) insists that a proper understanding of the cardinal virtues and theological virtues provide Catholics with an undergirding of spiritual formation (p. 227). Coupling the theological virtues and the cardinal virtues as components for developing a holistic spiritual framework will lead to healthy Christian ethics and integrity (McBrien, p. 228).

Finally, Bishop Emeritus Pilarczyk (1986) finds that there are thirteen "building blocks" for attuning a young person's spirituality to God: (1) faith, (2) hope, (3) love, (4) friendship, (5) family, (6) civil society, (7) work, (8) prayer, (9) church, (10) suffering, (11) aging, (12) death, and (13) liturgy. These thirteen areas encompass a comprehensive spirituality, which is "living in the Lord, responding to the holiness that God has already given [Christians] brings Christ out of the back room and into every aspect of [human] existence" (p. 3). It is clear that various spiritual traits can be taught, integrated, and practiced within a youth ministry, whether Catholic, Orthodox, Protestant, or Evangelical.

## The 2003 National Study of Youth and Religion

The National Study of Youth and Religion, which was published under the title *Soul Search: the Religious and Spiritual Lives of American Teenagers* by Christian Smith with Melinda Lundquist Denton (2005) investigated the faith lives, religious practices, and spiritual beliefs of thousands of American adolescents. This study is extremely helpful in shedding light on adolescent spirituality among American adolescents. Smith and Denton's findings regarding Catholic teenagers are quite sobering and warrant serious attention.[8] The implications for Catholic youth ministry are clear: Catholic adolescents are religiously weak and spiritually anemic. There is a laxity among Catholic adolescents and this "spiritual slackness" is directly connected to spirituality (p. 207).

Smith and Denton used interviews with three Catholic teenagers, Heather, John, and Alano, from different parts of the country to illustrate common themes they encountered in the religious lives of Catholic teenagers. All three reflected apathy, relaxed morality, openness to pre-marital sex, and irregular participation in Sunday Mass. If such teens are typical, they can "hardly [be] what the Catholic Church hopes for and expects of its [young] faithful" (p. 199). In fact, their answers to basic faith and ethical questions were appalling and difficult for any Catholic youth worker to read. Perhaps one of the most revealing findings of the study is that Catholic parents' own religiosity is weak and inconsequential to their own lives, which influences their teenagers. Smith and Denton (2005) note, "The relatively lower levels of Catholic teen religiosity simply reflect relatively low levels of Catholic parent religiosity. Perhaps the issue is not U.S. Catholic teen religious practice at all, but overall U.S. Catholic religious practice generally, as engaged and modeled by adults" (p. 208). From the NSYR there is really no doubt that parent(s) play a significant role in the lives of U.S. Catholic teenagers who deserve a strong Catholic spirituality and identity, but are not receiving it properly. There is little doubt that Catholic adolescents are easily bored with Catholic Sunday worship and that youth liturgical participation and Mass attendance are low, especially compared with mainline Protestant adolescents, which again, can be explained by lower levels of religiosity practiced by their (Catholic) parents (Smith and Denton, p. 210).

Tomás V. Sanabria (2007) follows up the research presented in NSYR and concentrates on Hispanic adolescent faith trends. His findings are similar to those of Smith and Denton (2005), but do reveal a few significant differences between Hispanic and non-Hispanic adolescents. Sanabria (2007) observes:

> 30 percent of Hispanic Catholic teens who feel extremely close to God have never made a [deep] commitment to God;

33 percent of the Hispanic Catholic respondents have had an experience of spiritual worship that was very moving and powerful;

61 percent of Hispanic Catholic teens . . . believe that God is a personal being involved in the lives of people today. (pp. 60-62)

Hispanic Catholic adolescents are not necessarily overtly spiritual. However, Sanabria (2007) notes that Catholic adolescents in general and Hispanic Catholics in particular may be spiritual in ways that do not fit the criteria [9] that NSYR used in its research.

First, most devout Hispanic Catholics may be choosing not to participate in their parish's youth [ministry] because it is *not religious enough for them.*

Second, it has already been shown [NSYR] that Catholics are less likely than Protestants to engage in Scripture study. Third, Hispanic Catholics tend to be much less individualistic about their faith than Hispanic Protestants. (p. 70)

This material indicates that Hispanic Catholics are spiritual, but might not be seen as spiritual because they do not adhere to the typical spiritual guidelines set forth by the NSYR or Caucasian stereotypes. As Sanabria (2007) notes, for most Hispanic Catholics, devotion, prayer, and religious celebrations happen at home around family and close friends (p. 70). Adolescent Hispanic Catholics may also have a stronger affinity for religious practices and rituals such as the Rosary and Stations of the Cross[10] -two ways that Catholic adolescents can enhance personal spirituality.

Clearly, from the results of NSYR and *Soul Searching*, a definitive paradigm shift needs to be made in the ministerial approach that the U.S. Catholic Church utilizes for its young people. The writing is on the wall. If the U.S. Catholic Church does not begin to increase the resources it puts into quality education, youth ministry, and adolescent programs, then an entire generation of Catholic adolescents' spirituality may be misguided, misplaced, or lost entirely. The cultivation of adolescent spirituality deserves to be one of the highest priorities of the Catholic Church and for the parents of young people. Therefore, comprehensive youth ministry must flourish in every parish in order to move Catholic youth from apathy about spiritual matters toward authentic transformation and religious awareness.

## Summary

Cultivating adolescent spirituality deserves to be a major concern and pastoral priority for the U.S. Catholic Church. Adolescent spirituality develops self-awareness in teenage faith life, moral life, spiritual life, and community life. Strengthening adolescent spirituality provides young people with opportunities for acknowledging, fostering, and celebrating adolescent identity and spirituality. A spirituality that caters to Catholic teenagers is never limited to age, grade, or gender, and is open to everyone from every ethnicity and culture. The attraction, implementation, and pastoral success of concentrating on bolstering adolescent spirituality in Catholic young people will rest in the competent hands of spiritually attuned youth ministers and parents.

*Renewing the Vision* strongly states, "If we are to succeed, we must offer young people a *spiritually challenging* and *world-shaping vision* that meets their hunger for the chance to *participate in a worthy adventure*" (p. 10). The challenge is great; therefore, our efforts and response as a U.S. Catholic Church must be equally great. We must encourage, empower, and equip Catholic adolescents with the skills to thrive as spiritual young people — this is a noble quest.

## Discussion Questions

(1) Describe the type of spirituality you had as a teenager, back in the day... What did it look like? What did it entail? What were your experiences?

(2) According to the U.S. Catholic Bishops' document — *Renewing the Vision* — what does Catholic adolescent spirituality entail for comprehensive Catholic youth ministry?

(3) Clarify the various types of spirituality that are made available to young people in your parish. How can adolescents experience spirituality in your parish?

(4) Review Shelton's four adolescent spirituality foci: Christ-centered, relational, future-oriented, and developmental and discuss which one is important to you. Explain your rationale.

(5) If you had no budget restraints or money was not an issue, envision the ways you would strengthen adolescent spirituality in the Catholic young people of your parish. In other words, what does your ideal, spiritually-infused youth ministry look like?

## CHAPTER THREE

# STRENTHENING EUCHARISTIC SPIRITUALITY IN CATHOLIC ADOLESCENTS

*"We think that we have every reason to have confidence in Christian youth: youth will not fail the Church if within the Church there are enough older people able to understand it, love it, guide it, and open up to it a future by passing on to it with complete fidelity the truth which endures. . . . And this is why we are pleased to dedicate more expressly to you, the young Christians of the present day, the promise of the Church of tomorrow, this celebration of spiritual joy."*[11]

**Pope Paul VI**
*1975, On Christian Joy*

As aforementioned, cultivating Christian spirituality in Catholic adolescents is not a new idea, but strengthening Eucharistic spirituality in Catholic teenagers may be. This chapter is occupied with the cultivation of individual spirituality within adolescents and with the cultivation of communal liturgical awareness and Eucharistic spirituality in Catholic teenagers. The focus will be to help enrich Eucharistic spirituality within young people approximately ages 13-18 years old or middle adolescence.

The chief aim of this chapter is twofold: (1) identify three ways that adolescents can deepen their Eucharistic spirituality in the context of Catholic comprehensive[12] youth ministry and (2) provide the merits for developing Eucharistic spirituality in lives of American Catholic adolescents.

## Enhancing Eucharistic Spirituality in Teenagers

Enhancing Eucharistic spirituality in adolescents can be a bit of a misnomer because the major ecclesial documents pertaining to youth ministry do not mention "Eucharist spirituality" by name; in fact the term "spirituality," rarely appears. The church literature relevant to youth ministry uses the phrase "prayer and worship."

As previously mentioned, *Renewing the Vision* is the blueprint for Catholic youth ministry is the United States. The document maintains that prayer and worship is vital for the spiritual lives of juvenile Catholics. RTV states,:

> The ministry of prayer and worship celebrates and deepens young people's relationship with Jesus Christ through the bestowal of grace, communal prayer and liturgical experiences; it awakens their awareness of the Spirit at work in their lives; it incorporates young people more fully into the sacramental life of the Church, especially Eucharist; it nurtures the personal prayer life of young people; and it fosters family rituals and prayer. (p. 44)

RTV provides the backdrop for adults who minister to adolescents to fully explore the opportunities to empower adolescents to become liturgically and Eucharistically spiritual.

There are only a handful of ways in which a person can heighten or stimulate Eucharistic spirituality. The predominant ways to enhance Eucharistic spirituality within adolescents, from my personal experience of being involved in Catholic youth ministry for twenty-five years include the following: (1) Sunday Eucharist, (2) Liturgy of the Hours, and (3) Eucharistic Exposition and Benediction. These three ways will be considered in the context of Catholic comprehensive youth ministry.

## Vibrant Sunday Eucharist

The most obvious way to boost Eucharistic spirituality in teenagers is the full participation in celebration of Sunday Eucharist, which is the climax of the Catholic weekly worship experience. The Second Vatican Council (1963) document, *Sacrosanctum Concilium*, expresses the importance of adolescents being attuned to Sunday Eucharist: "The liturgy is the summit toward which the activity of the Church is directed; at the same time it is the font from which all her power flows" (n. 10). Despite their cerebral comprehension of Sunday worship, Catholic teenagers are often "turned off" by the Sunday liturgy due to several reasons such as adolescent angst, preaching that fails to address youth's issues and concerns, music that does not captivate teenagers' religious imagination, and little (or no) liturgical catechesis preceding Sunday Eucharist. In order for Sunday Eucharist to be attractive to adolescents and to empower their spirituality, the celebration must be vibrant.

The National Federation for Catholic Youth Ministry (1997) document, *From Age to Age: the Challenge of Worship with Adolescents* notes,

> Many youth are not present at our parish worship. Many others are present but feel alienated from the group. This is the source of our concern and the reason for our action. As a community, we are less complete when these teens are not with us. When these adolescents are not visible and their voices are not heard at the liturgy, we are less able

> to give thanks and glory for the good works that God accomplishes through us. (p. 28)

Therefore greater effort placed upon youth participation and on cultivating Eucharistic spirituality may be pastorally prudent on the part of pastors and youth ministers.

NFCYM (1997) offers eight principles for vibrant worship with adolescents: (1) it *celebrates* their involvement in the Church's life and mission; (2) it *invites* and *accepts* their authentic participation; (3) it *attends* to the diversity of ages and cultures in the assembly; (4) it *roots* and *fosters* their personal prayer relationship with God; (5) it *includes* effective preaching of the word of God; (6) it has a youthful spirit in music and song; (7) it *incorporates* visually dynamic symbols and actions; and (8) it has an interactive and communal dimension (pp. 43-51). These eight ideals provide an enriching framework of vibrant Sunday worship with adolescents, and taken together, are to be woven into the fabric of comprehensive youth ministry. It may be wise to remember the words of the U.S. Catholic Bishops' Committee on the Liturgy (1982) document, *Music in Catholic Worship*: "Faith grows when it is well expressed in celebration. Good celebrations foster and nourish faith. Poor celebrations may weaken and destroy [faith]" (n. 6). Pastors, liturgists, and youth ministers who truly want to strive to increase Eucharistic spirituality in adolescents would be wise to foster vibrant (not necessarily contemporary, "folksy," or chaotic), but respectful music, and celebrate Sunday Eucharist that challenges and meets the teenager's worldview.

### *Pastoral Strategies*

There are several pastoral strategies for enhancing Eucharistic spirituality in adolescents that the parish leadership can easily implement.

> **First**, gather a sample representation of the youth in the parish for a "gathering session" or "town hall meeting" to discuss Sunday worship and

listen to the adolescents in the parish and their ideas, desires, and needs for Sunday Eucharist.

**Second**, study liturgical catechesis regarding the Eucharistic Prayers that are prayed during Sunday Mass, and teach the prayers' importance for Catholic spirituality and identity. They should be studied in religious education classes and youth ministries.

**Third**, promote and encourage young people to serve in a variety of parish liturgical ministries that allow them the opportunity to become apprenticed and mentored by an adult liturgical minister.

**Fourth**, celebrate liturgies well and with gusto, especially when youth are present in the assembly, because adolescents, like adults and children, are catechized by their liturgical experiences and sacramental encounters.

**Fifth**, promote other liturgical experiences within the liturgical tradition of the Catholic Church and then offer spiritual connections that reinforce the significance of Sunday Eucharist.

For adolescents to truly enjoy Sunday Eucharist, liturgies should engage, inspire, and relate to young people, and in this way the parish is fostering Eucharistic spirituality. Teenagers, like adults, yearn for meaningful and motivational preaching as well as soul-stirring and inspirational music.

## Liturgy of the Hours

In my twenty-five years of being involved in Catholic youth ministry, it is safe to state that Liturgy of the Hours (LOH) is the most *underutilized* liturgy that youth ministers celebrate and/or encourage with their youth. There are a number of reasons for this, but in large part because LOH is misunderstood, difficult to follow, and not youth-minister friendly in terms of a prayer text. Nevertheless, LOH, I have discovered over the years, is a great benefit to the adolescent ministry of prayer and worship, and it does empower Eucharistic spirituality among teenagers.

The revised *General Instruction to the Liturgy of the Hours* (1971) proclaims, "To the different hours of the day the Liturgy of the Hours extends the praise and thanksgiving, the memorial of the mysteries of salvation, the petitions and the foretaste of heavenly glory that are present in the Eucharistic mystery, 'the center and high point in the whole life of the Christian community'" (n. 12). LOH is the prayer of praise and petition, the prayer of Christ, the prayer of the Church, and the action of the Holy Spirit (no. 2, 8).

Therefore, LOH is an excellent expression of public worship for adolescents to strengthen their Eucharistic spirituality by: (1) learning about its rich history from Jewish antecedents (n. 100); (2) understanding its official status in the church as a "prayer of praise and petition" (n. 2); (3) valuing its ability to sanctify time and human activity (n. 11); (4) experiencing LOH in youth ministry settings in order that young people may benefit spiritually from celebrating LOH regularly (n. 12); and (5) participating in LOH on their own at home individually or as a family in order that teenagers grow in holiness and in Christian maturity (n. 14).

Catholic pastors and youth ministers would be wise to introduce LOH as a genuine and routine part of creating an ambiance of prayer and worship with adolescents. In earlier NFCYM (1986) document, *The Challenge of Adolescent Catechesis: Maturing in Faith* remarks, "Prayer and worship are an integral component of addressing adolescent spirituality. This faith theme [prayer and worship] helps older adolescents develop a personally-held spirituality and a rich personal and communal prayer life" (p. 85). Cultivating Eucharistic spirituality in adolescents means developing and sustaining their interior life.

## Pastoral Strategies

Strategies for integrating LOH and developing a young person's spiritual life may include this non-exhaustive list.

**First**, teach teenagers about the nature and purpose of prayer, and the impact that prayer makes upon a Christian.

**Second**, youth ministers may want explore the Church's understanding of liturgical prayer — LOH, Mass, RCIA rites, and penance services — as distinct from private prayer.

**Third**, youth ministers may find it beneficial to gather a small group of core students and adult youth leaders (volunteers) to read and discuss the GILOH text and "break it open" for its liturgical theology and pastoral applications.

**Fourth**, that same small group could plan a celebration of LOH and implement the liturgy in the youth ministry, ideally with a priest or deacon presiding over the celebration (albeit not absolutely necessary).

**Fifth**, expose young people to variations of LOH such as preparing LOH worship aids to take with on retreats, diocesan youth conferences, mission trips, national youth conferences, and World Youth Day, which will provide adolescents with a deeper and richer prayer experience.

While celebrating LOH at Saint Patrick's Cathedral, Pope John Paul II (1979) declared, "The value of the Liturgy of the Hours is enormous! Through [LOH] all the faithful fulfill a role of prime importance: Christ's prayer goes on in the world." Young people are called no less to help fulfill the universal call to holiness, live as Christian disciples, and to experience the richness of communal prayer.

## Eucharistic Exposition and Benediction

Eucharistic Exposition and Benediction has become increasing popular among Catholic teenagers in the United States. The rise in Eucharistic Exposition and Benediction is due in large part because many Catholic youth ministry organizations and adolescent pastoral movements are extremely enthusiastic about celebrating Eucharistic Exposition and Benediction. The overwhelming majority of youth ministers and adolescents refer to exposition of the Blessed Sacrament as "Eucharistic adoration." Albeit those familiar with the rite know that "adoration" is but one element within the ritual.[13]

Eucharist Exposition and Benediction is an excellent way to strengthen Eucharistic spirituality for several reasons.[14] First and foremost, Eucharistic veneration should help to lead Catholics to a fuller and more fruitful participation in Sunday Eucharist. Second and simultaneously, Eucharistic adoration is another rich worship experience to which teenagers should be exposed. The USCCB (2004) document, *Thirty-One Questions on Adoration of the Blessed Sacrament* states,

> The celebration of the Most Holy Eucharist is, certainly, the "fount and apex" of the entire Christian life. Yet the "spiritual life . . . is not limited solely to participation in the liturgy." Pope John Paul II calls worship of the Most Holy Eucharist outside Mass "an important daily practice [that] becomes an inexhaustible source of holiness" and practice "of inestimable value for the life of the Church." (p. 1, q. 1)

Clearly Eucharistic veneration exerts great influence on fostering the devotional life of Catholics and such devotion can extend the zeal for prayer and service to the Church's ministries.

Third and theologically, Eucharistic worship apart from the Sunday assembly has its roots in Sunday liturgy itself and in the sacrifice of the Mass. Catholic sacramental theologian John H. McKenna (1990) comments that any Eucharistic veneration has the same real presence, first in meal-sharing and second, by the "law of extension," whereby the Eucharistic elements are sacramental, spiritual, and symbolic realities and extensions of the liturgical act itself (p. 28). The ritual text *Holy Communion and Worship of the Eucharist Outside of Mass* (1973) observes, "When the faithful adore Christ present in the sacrament, they should remember that this presence derives from the sacrifice and has as its purpose both sacramental and spiritual communion" (no. 80). Consequently, the ultimate purpose of Eucharistic devotion in youth ministry settings is to help young people further share in the paschal mystery of Jesus the Christ.

Fourth and foundationally, good liturgical theology and practice should always flow from the liturgical rites themselves as the ancient Latin axiom attributed to Prosper of Aquitaine (390-455 C.E.), *lex orandi, lex credendi* (the law of prayer is the law of belief), maintains. Therefore, it may be worthwhile for youth ministers to read and examine the rite pertaining to Eucharistic Exposition and Benediction. The great medieval theologian and doctor of the Catholic Church, Saint Thomas Aquinas (1224-1274), observes,

> And since in all acts of [worship] that which is *without* is referred to that which is *within* as being of greater import, it follows that exterior adoration is offered on account of interior adoration. In other words, [Christians] exhibit signs of humility in our bodies in order to incite our affections to submit to God, since it is connatural to us to proceed from the sensible to the intelligible" (ST, IIa-IIae, q. 84, a. 2, p. 1547; italic added).

For Saint Thomas Aquinas, exterior Eucharistic veneration takes place because of the interior affection and admiration that the Christian bestows on Jesus the Christ.

### *Pastoral Strategies*

It may prove quite sensible for youth ministers and adult youth leaders in a parish to study and learn about Eucharistic theology and Eucharistic veneration before actually integrating Eucharistic Exposition and Benediction into parish ministry settings. There are three simple suggestions that youth ministers and adult youth leaders in ministry may want to seriously consider.

> **First**, a thorough reading of the document HCWEOM (1973) should empower youth ministers and adult youth leaders with a deeper understanding of Eucharistic Exposition and Benediction. Ideally, such a reading may also encourage parish ministers to read other ecclesial documents on the Eucharist. In addition, lay ministers may find themselves better equipped to deal with questions and issues that surround the Eucharist.
>
> **Second**, there must be appropriate catechesis on Eucharistic adoration as *distinct* from Sunday Eucharist — this is paramount! On the one hand, a clear and intentional distinction should be made with the people about the full celebration of Sunday Eucharist, in which the focal points are the **altar, ambo,** and **presider chair**, and on the other, the various forms of Eucharistic devotion, in which the focal points are the tabernacle and either the monstrance or ciborium containing the reserved sacrament[15]. One pastoral recommendation is to offer a retreat that centers on the celebration of Sunday Eucharist.[16]

**Third**, Eucharistic adoration in and of itself may be considered a passive activity and private devotion, even when celebrated within the context of community; therefore, every effort should be made to *assimilate* **adoration** *with* **action**, which is the pinnacle purpose of celebrating Sunday Eucharist. Theologically, Eucharistic adoration is best celebrated when it leads to Christian action, which is tantamount to Christian service and outreach, social justice initiatives, works of charity, and works of mercy. Sunday Eucharist by its very nature leads to Christian service, not passive receptivity, and no Eucharistic celebration should ever be perceived as passive or as liturgical entertainment. Eucharistic liturgies ideally should always lead to Christian action, service, and witness. One pastoral recommendation that is especially geared for youth ministry is to have young people assemble as a youth community at the cathedral parish, which represents the flagship church of the diocese.[17]

There are many possibilities that can be explored for helping teenagers become more spiritually attuned by exposing them to the rite of Eucharistic Exposition and Benediction. Fittingly, adolescents may need some coaching from their parish priest on the ways that a meditative contemplation of Christ in the Blessed Sacrament can be linked to the actual celebration of Sunday Eucharist and to the reception of Holy Communion (Driscoll, p. 89).

## Summary

Whether strengthening Eucharistic spirituality by participating in the full celebration of Sunday Eucharist, praying the Liturgy of the Hours, or contemplating Christ in the Blessed Sacrament through Eucharistic Exposition and Benediction, these three rituals will definitely enhance adolescent faith.

Beyond providing opportunities for youth to have direct exposure to sacred liturgies, NFCYM (1997) suggests the following to bolster spirituality in young people: (1) intentional catechesis, (2) liturgical catechesis, (3) the community's response, (4) opportunities for service, (5) retreats, days of reflection, and days of formation, (6) family catechesis, (7) a variety of faith experiences, (8) catechist formation, (9) collaboration, and (10) diverse prayer and worship experiences (pp. 40-43). These pastoral initiatives will benefit adolescents' spirituality because they help to foster a deeper understanding and appreciation of liturgy, prayer, and worship in the Catholic tradition.

Cultivating Eucharistic spirituality in adolescents can take various forms, but the three that are described in this chapter seem most appropriate for four reasons: (1) they are official liturgies of the Catholic Church, (2) they have their own ritual text and rubrics to follow, (3) they follow and adhere to the U.S. Catholic Bishops' vision of youth ministry as stipulated in RTV (1997), and (4) they foster a communal worship experience and individual liturgical spirituality in adolescents. As the GILOH (1971) states, "There is special excellence in the prayer of the community" (n. 9), which the liturgical celebrations of Sunday Eucharist, Liturgy of the Hours, and Eucharistic Exposition and Benediction help to encourage.

It may be noteworthy to recall that the hallmark of *all* Catholic liturgies celebrated with young people is for them to become the light of Christ, through the process of regeneration at baptism, and to become *little christs* (with a small "c") through the weekly celebration of Sunday Eucharist, and through other sacred encounters with God and the risen Christ. It is never too early to instill in young Catholics that, as Catholics, we become that which we believe, celebrate, and receive. In the famous words of Saint Augustine of Hippo (354-430 C.E.), who remarks: "If, therefore, you are the body of Christ and his members, *your* mystery has been placed on the Lord's Table, *you* receive your mystery. You reply 'Amen' to that which you are, and by replying your consent. . . Be what you see, and receive what you are" (Sermon 272).[18] Strengthening Eucharistic spirituality is an awesome responsibility of parents and the Church, but it is also a real blessing!

## Discussion Questions

(1) Before reading this chapter what was your idea of strengthening Eucharistic spirituality? Do you recall if your spirituality was impacted through Sunday Eucharist (Mass) as a teenager?

(2) Describe your parish's Sunday Eucharistic liturgies (Mass): Are they youth-friendly? Would you consider them vibrant? Does the effectiveness of the preaching reach out to the adolescents in the pews? Is the music both appealing and spiritually uplifting for the youth?

(3) Have you ever heard of the Liturgy of the Hours? What is your experience of Liturgy of the Hours? Think of the ways in which the youth ministry of your parish could incorporate Liturgy of the Hours.

(4) Discuss the significance of this statement: "Eucharistic adoration should help to lead Catholics to a fuller and more fruitful participation in Sunday Eucharist." What exactly does this say to you?

(5) Review the Eucharistic Exposition and Benediction section and discuss the pastoral strategies. Which one is most suitable for the youth of your parish to experience? Explain your reasoning.

*Chapter Four*

# The Usefulness of 12 Pastoral Practices for Cultivating Spirituality in Catholic Adolescents

> *"What is needed today is a Church which knows how to respond to the expectations of young people. Jesus wants to enter into dialogue with them and, through his body which is the Church, to propose the possibility of a choice which will require a commitment of their lives. As Jesus with the disciples of Emmaus, so the Church must become today the traveling companion of young people."*[19]
>
> **Pope John Paul II**
> *1995, World Youth Day*

Cultivating adolescent spirituality is of major interest to the U.S. Catholic Bishops (RTV, p. 20) and the 12 *virtues, traits, practices,* and *disciplines* that will be identified in this section will help to accomplish that end. I will use the aforementioned four terms interchangeably throughout this chapter. These 12 Catholic practices derive from both common pastoral praxis and from spiritual disciplines over the ages, but due to the parameters of this essay, they will only be briefly addressed. This section is informed by my own experiences and work in Catholic youth ministry spanning a 25-year period. Over the years I have witnesses thousands adolescents and observed hundreds of hours of young people trying become more spiritually attuned to God.

Moreover, during my 25 years of adolescent ministry experience, I have found these 12 traits and practices predominantly useful in strengthening spirituality in adolescents. Although none of these 12 virtues and disciplines is new to Christian spirituality, they offer the juvenile worker or youth minister a pragmatic perspective to employ in their work as well as offer a valuable synthesis of existing material. The 12 areas are designed to be integrated into the faith life of Catholic teenagers as pragmatic pastoral skills that enrich and enliven their faith journey seeking the Christian triune God. The 12 virtues and practices are listed alphabetically and not by any particular order or level of importance: (1) Bible time, (2) contemplation, (3) honesty, (4) introspection, (5) journaling, (6) meditation, (7) music, (8) prayer, (9) retreats, (10) Rosary, (11) spiritual direction, and (12) time usage.

### 1. Bible Time

"From strength to strength" is an ancient biblical axiom (Psalms 84:7) that means human beings are capable of progressing from one success to another higher level of success. Growing in holiness or cultivating spirituality in adolescents resonates with the above adage. The author of Second Timothy comments on the merit of sacred Scripture, "All Scripture is inspired by God and is useful for teaching, for refutation, for correction, and for training in righteousness, so that one who belongs to God may be competent, equipped for every good work" (2 Timothy 3:16-17). There is no doubt that the Bible is the most treasured book within Christianity, and there is no reservation about its positive impact on spirituality.

The discipline of reading the Bible is an excellent way for teenagers to increase their spirituality. The NFCYM document (1986) maintains that Scripture deepens and nourishes adolescent faith. The document reads, "The catechesis for each faith theme is grounded in Scripture. This [scriptural] catechesis fosters in adolescents a deepening knowledge and appreciation of the other Scriptures in the Church's tradition and in their own lives" (p. 78). Adolescents can glean much spiritual wisdom and practical guidance from spending time in the word of God. Spending time in the word of God allows young people the opportunity for personal prayer and for personal catechesis, both of which are excellent ways to enhance their spirituality.

Scripture scholar Walter Brueggemann (1997) indicates that the Bible is best presented as an invitation and alternative for a juvenile to enjoy.

> The Bible provides [youth] with an alternative identity, an alternative way of understanding [themselves], an alternative way of relating to the world. [The sacred Scriptures] offer a radical and uncompromising challenge to [the] ordinary ways of self-understanding. [The word of God] invites [youth] to join in and to participate in the ongoing pilgrimage of those who live in the shattering of history, caring in ways which matter, secured by the covenanting God who is likewise on pilgrimage with [youth] in history. (p. 23)

Brueggemann provides compelling rationale for teenagers to be engaged with the Bible. Catholic teenagers could be encouraged to read and study the sacred Scriptures at home with their family, at church in their youth ministry, at school in a Bible study, and alone during their personal devotional time.

## 2. Contemplation

"Our lives are lived forward and understood backwards" is a Christian sentiment attributed to nineteenth century Danish philosopher Sören Kierkegaard (1813-1855), which helps to situate the intensity of contemplation. The Prophet Zechariah prophesied, "Not by power, not by might, but by my spirit, says the Lord of hosts" (Zechariah 4:6), which implies that God works in the stillness and quietness of the human heart. Franciscan theologian Ilia Delio (2005) affirms, "Contemplation is a penetrating gaze that gets to the heart of reality. It is looking into the depths of things with the eyes of the heart and seeing them in their true relation to God" (p. 132). The spiritual discipline of contemplation involves self-awareness, self-acceptance, and self-actualization, which all lead toward total Christian transformation (Canales, 2005b; Wright, 2000).

Contemplation is an experience of "being present" to God or "being caught up" with God. Contemplation is a deeper and more reflective prayer practice than both meditation and introspection. Contemplation requires and entails more silence, solitude, and stillness. William Shannon (1993) maintains that, "[Spiritual] awareness, which is central to contemplation, is a very different experience from [introspection]: it tends always to be unitive; [contemplation] cannot *be* apart from God" (p. 209). Contemplative prayer exercises work well with adolescents and are gaining in popularity with youth (Shelton, 1983; White, 2005; Yaconelli, 2006).

Contemplative prayer with youth is an invitation for adolescents to enter into a more meaningful relationship with the triune God. There are two ancient Catholic contemplative practices that can be adjusted to fit a youth ministry curricula: (1) *lectio divina* and (2) centering prayer (Yaconelli, 2006; pp. 84-89). Thomas Keating (1993) comments, "Centering prayer is a method designed to facilitate the development of contemplative prayer by preparing one's faculties to cooperate with this gift . . . it is not meant to replace other kinds of prayer; it simply puts other kinds of prayer into a new and fuller perspective" (p. 139). Centering prayer is also found in meditation (to be addressed later in this chapter) and in many respects is a simplified version of the *lectio divina*, and it is not an end in itself, but a beginning because it enjoys less "study" and "thinking" about God and concentrates on resting or relaxing and "being" in God's holy presence (Keating, 1993). Since contemplation is demanding for teenagers, it will be further explored in the next chapter.

## *3. Honesty*

"Honesty is the best policy" is a pithy phrase that parents train their children to use when telling the truth, and there is much veracity to its content. The fourth Gospel depicts Jesus of Nazareth as boldly proclaiming to his friends, "and you will know the truth, and the truth will set you free" (John 8:32). Although Jesus is concerned about discipleship in this periscope, he does mention the fruit of being honest. Honesty, also known as truth-telling, is always important to one's self-identity and self-discovery (Aden, 2005; p. 1288). Honesty can save one much aggravation and heartache. In terms of developing adolescent spirituality, it is best to take a long, hard look at one's spiritual life and simply assess its "worth" (Canales, 2004a; c 1). In other words, in which direction is the adolescent heading in terms of their spiritual quest (Canales, 2005a; pp. 10-11)? Is the youth merely interested in fun and games, dating, and eating pizza, or is the teenager seriously interested in enhancing Christian spirituality and discipleship (Canales, 2005a; pp. 10-11)? Being honest with one's self and with others is part of the metaphysical dimension of knowing, which leads to personal and communal insight.

Jesuit psychologist Charles M. Shelton (1983) states, "Because honesty is a critical aspect of [humanity] . . . [it should] be explored in various roles and relationships in the adolescent's life" (p. 275). Practicing the virtue of honesty is also an excellent way to encourage youth in self-reflection. Youth ministers may want to concentrate on specific content-filled experiences, roles, and relationships, and reflect with adolescents on their propensity for honesty, caring, and sensitivity (Shelton, p. 275).

Honesty is a virtue that certainly can capture an indwelling integrity of a person.

Canadian Jesuit theologian Bernard J.F. Lonergan (1904-1984) maintains that insight is reached through intellectual morality. Lonergan (1972) contends that seeking honesty is part of discerning God's will and is expressed in four categorical imperatives: (a) being attentive, (b) being intelligent, (c) being reasonable, and (d) being responsible (pp. 8-9). In Lonergan's (1958) schema, Christians gain wisdom and insight from being honest, a spiritual practice known as "discernment," which may include combinations of *empiricism* (honesty in experiences), *idealism* (honesty in concepts), and *realism* (honesty in judgments) (pp. 622-623). Honesty is an important virtue for cultivating spirituality in adolescent Christians because it is liked to a Gospel value (Canales, 2004a; c 1). Fostering honesty in Catholic adolescents is a worthwhile endeavor for three reasons: (a) it is character-building in youth and helps them to discern integrity, (b) it is a virtue laudable to promote and try to instill among adolescents, and (c) it helps the adult youth leaders who assess, evaluate, and facilitate youth programs to raise the conscious of youth (Shelton, p. 61).

## 4. Introspection

"To know thyself is divine" is a seventeenth century English expression that captures the essence of introspection. The Apostle Paul informs the early Church, "You must lay aside your former life . . . acquire a fresh, spiritual way of thinking" (Ephesians 4:22-23). Introspection can be a fresh and spiritual way of thinking for young Christians. Introspection is a fancy word for simply reflecting and looking inward. The practice of personal introspection in its simplest form is merely assessing one's life: sitting (or walking), thinking, pondering, and reflecting upon ways to continuously change one's life for the good, with the assistance of God. Ilia Delio (2004) likens introspection to "ascending" to God because it is a process by which Christians can go "inward to the core of who [they] are, [as] created them in the image of God" (pp. 23-24).

One spiritual method of personal introspection which might aid adolescents in their quest for cultivating spirituality is the "Examination of Conscience." The Examination provides adolescents with a tangible and realistic blueprint to review their day or their week. Teaching adolescents to integrate introspection is a positive discipline that will allow them to examine their conscience and actions. Catholic spiritual author Phyllis Zagano (2003) reports, that the purpose of teenagers engaging in introspection is twofold: (a) trying to find God in all things and (b) working to gain freedom to cooperate with God's will (p. 4). Therefore, enlivening spirituality in youth may require teenagers to integrate introspection into their lives.

One expression for implementing introspection in the lives of Catholic youth is during the end of a weekly or monthly youth ministry gathering: Have the teenagers gather in a quiet and sacred space and allow them time to reflect upon their week and month. The process should not take longer than 10 minutes. There can be a large group debriefing or small group sharing or notebooks can be handed out for journaling.

## 5. *Journaling*

"The pen is mightier than the sword" is a medieval proverb that resonates well with the pastoral practice and spiritual exercise of writing one's thoughts or prayers as distinct from speaking them and praying them verbally. The Psalmist writes "[Because] my heart is stirred by a noble cause, as I sing my ode to my [God]; my tongue is the pen of a nimble scribe" (Psalms 45:2). Writing down personal thoughts on paper in a diary-like fashion is an excellent pastoral evaluative tool that will allow a person to grow in spirituality.

Corita Clarke (1991) holds that journaling can be either a simple or complex method for teenagers to enrich and expand their spirituality.

> [Journaling] can be a reflection on one's prayer, on one's daily life, or both. In spite of some initial hesitation or resistance, most [young] people who

> are guided in the process of journaling find it beneficial. As one reflects in order to write, one taps into a deeper sub-conscious awareness and in the act of writing, releases this awareness and brings it to consciousness. (p. 51)

Adolescents may find that regular journaling will help them to discover patterns of God working in their lives and can record these interactions, and thus, keep a diary of God's promises. Journaling actively records a teenager's thoughts, actions, events, personal happenings, feelings, inhibitions, excitements, stimulations, and the results of such experiences.

Les Parrott (2000) identifies five ways that journaling can fortify teenage spirituality: (a) journaling intensifies adolescents' awareness about their innermost feelings about themselves; (b) spiritual writing assists teenagers in reflecting about their day in terms of connecting spirituality through everyday tasks and choices; (c) a daily diary affords a relatively objective account for juvenile spirituality and spiritual changes within their life; (d) a spiritual log provides young people with an avenue to explore and examine their spiritual "trouble spots" or "sticking points" that may be hassling their spirituality instead of enhancing their spiritual awareness; and (e) a spiritual diary should empower youth to discern spiritual behavior patterns that reveals and re-reveals God's unconditional love and mercy (p. 148). Journaling is a powerful tool for adolescents because it assists them in self-understanding and self-awareness, which is part of enriching youth spirituality.

## 6. *Meditation*

"Our hearts are restless until they rest in Thee" is an ancient adage from Saint Augustine of Hippo (354-430 C.E.) and it represents the goal of meditation. The Psalmist remarks, "Let the words of my mouth meet with your favor, keep the mediation of my heart before you" (Palms 19:15). The practice of meditation emphasizes a return to the heart and is crucial for achieving or "advancing" in spirituality, even for young people

(Delio, 2004; p. 58). Meditation with young people will be challenging because it is a more intense type of prayer, distinct from liturgical, rote, or spontaneous prayer forms, one that involves reflection and self-awareness (Freeman, 1993; p. 649). Meditation is a more intense than introspection, and one that involves reflection and self-awareness; however, it is not as demanding as contemplation, which requires that teenagers have a strong self-identity (Freeman, p. 650).

Techniques for involving adolescents in meditation could entail reflection on a single word or phrase like "It's no big deal, everything's going to be all right," or "Let go and let God." Meditation can also be reciting a simple mantra or chant such as "Praise you, God," "I love you Lord," or "God is great," or reflection on a New Testament pericope or meditating on a cross/crucifix, or a religious icon. This technique is called "centering prayer" because it focuses prayer in meditation (Canales, 2004a; c 1). These practices should begin for small amounts of time, e.g., one-minute and increase to five to 10 minutes per day, and realistically, young people should not be expected to pray more than adults.

Meditation for Catholic teenagers could also be as simple as reciting a prayer over and over that focuses the mind and heart upon God, such as the Hail Mary or the Glory Be. Since meditation is akin to contemplation, it, too, will be further addressed in the next chapter.

### 7. *Music*

"Singing is praying twice," is another ancient adage attributed to Saint Augustine of Hippo (354-430C.E.). It still speaks powerfully today because music, song, and lyrics are so much a part of adolescent life and culture. The Scripture passage "make a joyful noise to the Lord" (Psalm 66:1; 89:16) reflects the understanding that music and song help to nurture spirituality. Music is an excellent vehicle for cultivating teenage spirituality. The U.S. Catholic Bishops (1997) state, "Music is a significant part of personal expression for young people, and that desire carries over to their participation in liturgy" (RTV, 46). All adolescents listen to a favorite musical style and genre. The crucial element for those trying to help develop spirituality in adolescents is to tap into the musical styles, melodies, genres, and lyrics that capture the religious imagination of young people.

It is no great surprise that the average American adolescent listens to lots of music every day. Adolescent psychologists Philip Rice and Kim Dolgin (2005) report, "One study, which examined the listening habits of 2,700 14-to-16-year-olds; found that [teenagers] listened to music an average of 40 hours per week" (p. 324). Walt Mueller (2007) reports, "Recent studies put the estimates at more than five hours a day" (p. 88). The following observation regarding the music habits of adolescents (8-18 -year olds) provides evidence of the prevalence of music in adolescents' daily routines:

> 74 percent report listening to radio,
> 68 percent report listening to CD player or mp3,
> 99 percent of homes have CD/tape player,
> 20 percent view music via computer in their bedrooms,
> 58 percent listen to music while doing homework
>   (Mueller, 2007; p. 89).

There is absolutely no doubt that music not only entertains young people, but influences them and may even educate them as well.

Sociologist Christian Smith (2005) notes, "Between 20 and 29 percent of [adolescents] play religious music. . . and about one-third of teens report having listened to religious music outside of a concert . . . twenty percent of nonreligious teens, for instance, listen to religious music" (p. 47). This suggests that Christian music is impacting U.S. teenagers in significant numbers. Consequently, the importance of music for adolescent spirituality looms large because music has the potential to captivate young people as a spiritual medium.

Youth ministry educators Merton P. Strommen and Richard A. Hardel (2000) are convinced that, "Music is more important to today's young generation than it is to any other generation; songs that touch [adolescents] most are those that speak to their pain, their isolation, their experience" (p. 166). Music has the power to transform and move teenagers to a deeper spirituality. The NFCYM document (1997) states, "The music of the young brings freshness and variety to our current musical genres and can infuse sacred music with energy and vitality" (p. 49). Perhaps nothing inspires youth more than music; and these findings point to the fact that music occupies a vast amount of adolescent's time and is extremely relevant for youth culture. Nevertheless, youth ministers' greatest and most difficult task is to have parish communities integrate music that captures the hearts and imagination of young people, while at the same time, help youth to find the beauty and richness in the more traditional hymns of the Christian faith.

## *8. Prayer*

"Pray always and in all ways" is a slogan that has gained much attention in the past ten years within Christian circles, and it speaks to the significance of prayer. The Apostle Paul gives the Church a clear mandate to pray: "Pray without ceasing" (1 Thessalonians 5:17) and "With all prayer and supplication, pray at every opportunity in the Spirit" (Ephesians 6:18). Christians pray because Jesus was a person of prayer and thus modeled prayer for the Christian community. The discipline of prayer helps teenagers integrate their faith life and spirituality and to express their spirituality (Engebretson, 2004).

Albeit there are many prayer forms for adolescents to experience and which encourage spirituality, this subsection will discuss prayer laconically and generally. Prayer is language of the heart, and prayer in its simplest form is a human being communicating and interacting with God, and God communicating and interacting with a human being (Canales, 2004b; p. 39). Teaching young people to pray and offering a variety of prayer experiences (liturgical and non-liturgical; public and private; rote and spontaneous) empowers teenager's spirituality and heightens their experience of prayer, and allows them to enter into a more personal relationship with Jesus Christ. Kathleen Engebretson (2004) observes, "Prayer is used to express spirituality, but more commonly is a capacity for reflection, particularly through challenging activities" (p. 276). Prayer is an important dynamic of adolescent faith and fosters spiritual wholeness (White, 2005; p. 141).

The National Federation of Catholic Youth Ministry (1997) document titled *From Age to Age: the Challenge of Worship with Adolescents* discusses the importance of fostering the discipline of prayer in young people. Youth ministry programs which strengthen adolescent prayer also strengthen a juvenile's relationship with God (p. 46). The NFCYM (1997) document further notes, "Teens need opportunities and encouragement to voice spontaneous prayers, sing in groups, and bring their ideas and issues to community prayer" (p. 47). Providing an array of opportunities for adolescents to pray will allow them to encounter a "smorgasbord" of meaningful spiritual activities. RTV (1997) addresses prayer and its impact upon a juvenile's spirituality:

> The ministry of prayer and worship *celebrates* and *deepens* young people's relationship with Jesus Christ through the bestowal of grace, communal prayer and liturgical experiences; it *awakens* their [spiritual] awareness of the spirit at work in their lives; it *incorporates* young people more fully into the sacramental life of the Church, especially [Sunday] Eucharist; it *nurtures* the personal prayer life of young people; and it *fosters* family rituals and prayer. (p. 44)

The U.S. Catholic Bishops are clear that prayer is an essential component of effective Catholic youth ministry, and it also strengthens spirituality in teenagers. Prayer cannot be overlooked or underestimated-its value is supreme-various types of prayer and teaching teenagers to pray are quintessential to cultivating spiritually rich youth.

### 9. Retreats

"Let go and let God" is a popular Christian slogan that has appeared on t-shirts and bumper stickers, but it reminds young Christians that God orders human direction and that Christians are called to accept that divine direction. The Gospel of Luke states, "Filled with the Holy Spirit, Jesus retreated from the Jordon and was led by the Spirit into the desert for forty days" (4:1-2). Retreats are the spiritual practice of withdrawing from the usual rhythm and routine of daily life for the purpose of boosting adolescents' interior life. Retreats are part of the Christian tradition and are paramount in youth spiritual development. Retreats take people out of their "comfort zone" and allow them to concentrate on spiritual matters experience God's presence because they are removed from their everyday realities and stresses: school, sports, family, and peers. Canales (2002) notes, "Weekend retreats are the spiritual backbone of a quality parish-based youth ministry. From my experience teenagers love to participate in weekend retreats and are enthusiastic and excited about them" (p. 31). Notice that I specify weekend retreats as distinct from a one-day or half-day events, which are more likened to days of reflection, and in my experience, do not have the full catechetical and spiritual impact of a weekend or multiple-day retreat. Retreats are perhaps the greatest spiritual vehicle for youth workers to help cultivate spirituality in juveniles.

Catholic adolescent ministry scholar Michael Warren (1987) refers to retreats as Christian experience programs, "Most of the Christian experience programs I know about encourage those who have been on one weekend to come back to others in one or another capacity" (p. 133). The ultimate purpose of weekend retreats is to foster spirituality within the lives of young people as they encounter God. "A retreat increases the spirituality of a person, which enables them to come to a deeper understanding and appreciation of God and their personal relationship with God based upon their own experiences with God" (Canales, 2002; 31). These weekend spiritual experiences and encounters with God come in a variety of formats, and the names differ from diocese to diocese, but they are paramount to strengthening adolescent spirituality.

RTV (1997) discusses the importance of a solid retreat ministry: "Ministry with adolescents provides balance . . . [that] can be achieved throughout a year or a season of programming; even a single program or strategy can incorporate several of the ministry components, as in the case of a retreat program" (p. 26). Thomas East (2004) maintains that retreats serve as a medium for enhancing teenage spirituality. "Youth retreats have a unique ability to touch the hearts of young people . . . retreats have the power to change the lives of young people, calling them more deeply into discipleship" (p. 49). Those working with youth in a Christian context recognize the enormous transformational power that weekend retreats offer to young people.

## *10. Rosary*

The simple phrase attributed to Saint and Pope Pius X (1835-1914) states, "Of all prayers, the Rosary is the most beautiful and the richest in graces," sums up the Catholic belief in Mary of Nazareth (ca. 20 B.C.E.-40C.E.), the mother of Jesus of Nazareth. The Canticle of Mary (Luke 1:46-55) in the Christian Word of God indicates the role of Mary is significant to Christianity and is the scriptural basis of the Rosary (*rosarium* meaning "rose garden"). The spiritual discipline of praying the Rosary is a 1,000-year tradition, and it is a form of personal meditation that is taught to all Catholics, from toddlers through adulthood, and is encouraged as a meditative, non-liturgical, and private prayer form by the Catholic Church (Pope Paul VI, 1974; Pope John Paul II, 1987, 2002; *Catechism of the Catholic Church*, no. 2676-2679, 2708).

The Rosary consists of four mysteries: the joyful mysteries, the luminous mysteries, the sorrowful mysteries, and the glorious mysteries. Each "mystery" correlates with an aspect or event in Jesus' life and ministry. The foci of the prayers contained in the Rosary are Jesus Christ centered not Mariain in nature. The Rosary makes an excellent mediation exercise for adolescents because it is simple, straightforward, route, and creates an ambiance of silence and reflection. Youth ministers will find that praying the Rosary can bolster adolescent spirituality in youth and it does not take that mush planning or preparation to integrate into the ministry.

### *11. Spiritual Direction*

The pithy phrase "sometimes a-floatin'" and "sometimes a-fishin'" sums up the nature of Christian spiritual direction with adolescents. As the wisdom teacher in the Bible indicates, "Love to listen-you will gain much knowledge" is a good thing (Sirach 6:33). In other words, listening is a good discipline to engage in and can be beneficial. The spiritual practice of spiritual direction is an age-old practice that has taken place between pupils and spiritual guides who practice the art of holy listening. Catholic spiritual directors and Jesuits William A. Barry and William J. Connolly (1978) state, "Spiritual direction, as we understand it then, is directly concerned with a person's actual experience of [their] relationship with God" (p. 7). Compatible with these insights are the views of Catholic spiritual directors Francis K. Nemeck and Marie T. Coombs (1993) who maintain,

> Spiritual direction is a gift, and charism, the ministry of guiding a person in and through her/his . . . spiritual regeneration, deification, transformation. Spiritual direction is a God-willed contribution of one person to another's process of spiritualization, interiorization, and sanctification. (p. 16)

The practice of spiritual direction is a wonderful pastoral tool to help a young person enrich their personal spirituality.

Dori G. Baker (2005) indicates that the art of holy listening with adolescents and evoking youth testimonies through holy listening is tantamount to spiritual direction and is a powerful pastoral tool (p. 54). Current research on spiritual direction with adolescents is threefold: (a) a process which is guided by the Holy Spirit to take the lead in facilitating the direction exchange,

(b) is concerned with "being in touch" with the pneumatic characteristics that are in the heart, mind, soul, and body of the young person who seeks spiritual guidance, and (c) tries to create an ethos of holy listening (Gratton, 1993; p. 915; Baker, 2005; p. 54). Orthodox Bishop Joseph F. Purpura (2008) argues that spiritual direction with adolescents is a much urgent endeavor for the Christianity.

One of the greatest *needs* of our young people today is spiritual direction. Never before have I seen more young people seeking to better understand their faith, yet at the same time I have never sensed a greater *lack* of spiritual direction available to them. (p. 1)

This statement sounds all too familiar to those who minister to youth in the Catholic Church and is a real dichotomy in Catholic youth ministry: spiritual direction is needed, but there is a dearth of qualified spiritual directors (Purpura, 2008).

Episcopal spiritual director Clement Mehlman (2000) observes that some spiritual direction encounters with young people are comparable to the image of "sitting in a boat with a fishing companion, bobbling about on the pond, moving according to the wind's breath or gust, . . . sometimes a-floatin'" (p. 1). Other times, spiritual direction with youth involves things like "asking for clarification, paraphrasing, raising my voice with hesitancy at the end of statements, weaving together the threads with tentativeness to aid the directee's reflection-go a-fishin'" (p. 2). Spiritual direction with adolescents is holy listening and is significant to cultivating adolescent spirituality (Mehlman, 2000; Baker, 2005; Purpura, 2008). Since spiritual direction is vital to enhancing adolescent spirituality, it will be further explored in the next chapter.

## 12. Time Usage

"Time Is On My Side" is a popular 1970's Rolling Stones song that effectively summarizes an adolescent's attitude concerning their life span. Typically, young people feel invincible and that nothing bad will ever happen to them until it does happen (Lerner, 2002; pp. 96-97). The author of Ecclesiastes wisely observes, "There is an appointed time for everything, and a time for every affair under the heavens" (Ecclesiastes 3:1). Employing time management as a spiritual virtue means that adolescents, like adults, must learn to live in harmony with time constraints and balance time with their activities, school work, relationships, part-time jobs, and spirituality. NFCYM Executive Director, Robert J. McCarty (1994), indicates that the use of time is a factor that must be managed effectively and efficiently if it is going to help cultivate spirituality in young Christians (p. 65). The reality is that U.S. Christian teenagers are busy people and few are able, even if willing, to commit a block of time to develop their personal spirituality (Carotta, 2002; p. 30). The lack of time can become a negative factor for adolescents encountering the Sacred.

Diocesan Director of Cincinnati, Ohio, Sean Reynolds (2005) maintains that Catholic youth are engrossed with activities and are extremely busy despite their young age. Reynolds (2005) states, "Many Catholic young people are victims of 'option overload': a byproduct of living in an affluent society with an overabundance of athletic, educational, entertainment, social, and religious opportunities, many of which are positive, healthy, and enjoyable" (p. 53). American Catholic youth, like the majority of adolescents from industrialized countries, have hectic lives and hunger for a break in the action, a bit of solitude, and much needed balance in their lives (Yaconelli, 2005; p. 114). Time need not be a restrictive factor for young people. Perhaps a specific time may to be scheduled by youth to empower themselves toward renewal. In a culture of busyness, one helpful aim of bolstering adolescent spirituality is to put young people not only in touch with God, but to allow them the time to be in communion with God.

### Summary of the 12 Practices and Disciplines

Ultimately, these 12 spiritual traits for developing adolescent spirituality-Bible time, contemplation, honesty, introspection, journaling, meditation, music, prayer, retreats, Rosary, spiritual direction, and time usage — are connected to a desired outcome to assist adolescents in their noble quest for spirituality. Ideally these 12 disciplines help adolescents to develop a reasonable spirituality which moves young people closer toward Christian conversion, discipleship, and the universal call to holiness that is disciplined, self-reflective, and experiences a deeper union with the Christian triune God (Pope John Paul II, 1999; pp. 43-54).

## Summary

The late Jesuit religious writer Pierre Teilhard de Chardin (1960) eloquently states, "We are not human beings having a spiritual experience; we are spiritual beings having a human experience" (p. 67). Cultivating spirituality in adolescents fosters the human experience and engages the teenage faith journey. Thomas East (2004) notes that enriching adolescent spirituality is a priority within Catholic ministry, and spirituality is central to the events, gatherings, and strategies of a parish's ministry with youth; prayer, faith formation, inspiration, and witness are essential to effective youth ministry (p. 75). Catholic adolescents are spiritual people and deserve quality encounters that nurture their spirituality.

Cultivating spirituality in adolescents creates a process and ambiance which is characterized by broadening the spiritual horizons of young people and deepening their personal faith-life through a variety of activities and strategies. Developing adolescent spirituality should never be a leap of faith into the unknown, but a process that is calculated and enriching (McQuillan, 2004). Encouraging Christian spirituality in Catholic adolescents is an approach that provides young people with opportunities for acknowledging, fostering, and celebrating adolescent identity and faith (Crawford and Rossiter, 2004; Baker 2005).

Continual transformation is the ultimate goal of cultivating Christian spirituality in adolescents (Pope John Paul II, 1999). Developing adolescent spirituality leads to transformation and is the goal of all Christians. Teenagers will increase their spirituality best through religious experiences (Wright,

2000; McQuillan, 2004; Canales 2005b; Engebretson, 2006). Therefore, creating spiritual experiences for young people to encounter God and community is perhaps the finest way for teaching, learning, and experiencing adolescent spirituality. "Youth do not simply want to learn about God . . . youth want to feel God, experience God's love, and enter into God's presence" (Canales, 2005b; 73). In this way, adolescent transformation will be reached through cultivating spirituality in teenagers.

## Discussion Questions

(1) Do you recall the spiritual activities that you participated in as a teenager? Which disciplines did you practice that were addressed in this chapter?

(2) Describe your understanding of retreats as a spiritual tool. How often does your parish youth ministry offer weekend retreats for its young people? What spiritual value do you find in weekend retreats?

(3) Review the Bible time, prayer, and music sections in this chapter. Which one of these seems most appropriate to implement as a pastoral practice in your youth ministry?

(4) Review the introspection, mediation, and contemplation sections in this chapter. Which one of these seems most appropriate to implement as a pastoral practice in your youth ministry?

(5) Let's model one of the 12 spiritual practices here: Take out a sheet of paper and journal for ten minutes without stopping about something that is important to you as a Catholic. For instance, write about siblings, parents, family, marriage, divorce, Jesus, etc.

## CHAPTER FIVE

# THREE APPROPRIATE SPIRITUAL PRACTICES FOR CULTIVATING CATHOLIC ADOLESCENT SPIRITUALITY

*"Youth are not merely the future of the Church, but rather the young community of today's Church. Nonetheless, it is a frequent experience that they [the youth] do not always feel this way, but instead feel marginalized and overlooked."*[20]

**Prophetic Voices**
*1986, Encuentro Nacional Hispano de Pastoral*

This chapter has two aims: (1) to examine three spiritual practices that are pastorally and developmentally appropriate and accessible for middle adolescents, and (2) to present the strengths and limitations of cultivating adolescent spirituality as the primary focus of youth ministry. The organization and the sequence of the areas being examined are straightforward and simple. The rationale here is that it is important to define and describe Catholic adolescent spirituality before addressing the three spiritual practices (meditation, contemplation, spiritual direction) for ministry with adolescents, and finally, provide the benefits and concerns for the praxis of strengthening spirituality in Catholic young people. Each section has subsections that identify and further clarify each of the main three sections of this chapter for addressing adolescent spirituality and assessing the three spiritual practices for adolescents in the U.S. Catholic Church.

In light of the definition of adolescent spirituality, its placement within comprehensive Catholic youth ministry, and the findings from the National Study of Youth and Religion, there are certain spiritual practices that are challenging, but are appropriate methods for enhancing adolescent spirituality in Catholics. There are three spiritual approaches that might be considered challenging for adolescents: (1) meditation, (2) contemplation, and (3) spiritual direction. However, these methods are perfectly acceptable theologically, psychologically, and developmentally for "middle" adolescents, ages 15 to 18.[12] These three spiritual practices are spiritual tools that lead teenagers to a deeper personal relationship with God. The next section is the bulwark of this chapter and concentrates on helping Catholic adolescents foster an ardent sense of Christian spirituality. Each section offers several activities or techniques to foster the particular spiritual practice and method that a youth minister may integrate with Catholic juveniles.

Catholic sociologist David J. Tacey (2004) writes about youth, cultural crisis, and eco-spirituality in his work *The Spirituality Revolution: The Emergence of Contemporary Spirituality*. Tacey remarks,

> I continue to be impressed by the vitality and strength of youth spirituality, and its astonishing appearance in the midst of a secular education system that does not encourage it, a religious system that does not understand it, and a materi-

alist society that gives no official sanction to it. It is in youth culture that we see the revolution most powerfully and persuasively at work; here we recognize that Western civilization is in transition, and that our institutional structures are out of date and unable to cope with the spirit of the new. (p. 175)

In Tacey's scheme, youth are developing their own brand of spirituality and are capable of divergent and alternative expressions of spiritual life, but they may need direction and sensitivity from adults. As a way to help young people express their spirituality more fully and encounter God on a deeper level, I propose the three aforementioned spiritual practices to cultivate adolescent spirituality, which are based on current adolescent ministry research. It is the intention of this author to recommend that Catholic youth ministers try these spiritual practices and integrate them regularly into comprehensive Catholic youth ministry.

## The Spiritual Practice of Meditation

Meditation is a more intentional prayer form than most other types of prayer. Meditation stems from the Hebrew word *haga*, which literally means "heart," and the Greek expression of meditation derives from the term *melete*, meaning "care, study, exercise"; therefore, meditation emphasizes a return to the heart or a caring for the heart (Delio 2004, p. 58; Freeman 1993, p. 648). Meditation is crucial for achieving or "advancing" in spirituality, but may be difficult for middle adolescents to master.

Benedictine monk Laurence Freeman (1993) maintains, "Meditation is a mental exercise and is distinct from spontaneous prayer or rote prayer and is more akin to a mantra, which can be a continuous repetition of thought or word that focuses the attention beyond thought and imagination and leads to a still, wakeful presence to the reality of God" (p. 649). Meditation is a more intense type of prayer, one that involves reflection and integrity, which requires that teenagers have a somewhat developed self-identity. Despite the wherewithal that adolescents need for authentic meditation, there are a variety of meditations that are age-appropriate and available for Catholics in middle adolescence: (1) reciting simple prayers and/or repeating over and over a simple phrase such as "Lord, I love you, and I want to make you happy," or "Come, Lord Jesus into my life," or "Come, Holy Spirit and enkindle into my life a fire,"; (2) drawing, coloring, or painting while simultaneously praying a certain prayer repeatedly; (3) journaling or creating a personal prayer while listening to Christian or classical music; (4) praying while looking at a crucifix, icon, or Christian image; and (5) praying the Rosary. Although these meditation practices might not entice all Catholic young people, they are worth trying.

Mark Yaconelli (2005) comments that meditation is like "listening to crickets" chirp because it requires the sensitivity to know that crickets can be heard and the maturity to quiet one's self to listen to them chirp (pp. 35-36). Meditation with adolescents involves listening, deepening one's awareness of God, and attending to one's experience of God. Mediation with adolescents aims, "in particular, [at] emphasizing the nearness of God, our relatedness to Christ, and the inspiration (in-spiriting) of the Holy Spirit empowering us for acts of mercy, justice, and peace in the world" (Yaconelli, 2005; p. 22). Albeit meditation is private and may be considered a passive enterprise, it should always galvanize one to awareness and action. Meditation has a close symbiotic connectedness with three prayerful activities that can be explored with adolescents: (1) introspection, (2) examination of consciousness, and (3) discernment.

### *1. Introspection*

Franciscan scholar Ilia Delio (2004) compares introspection to "ascending" to God because it is a process by which Christians can go "inward to the core of who [they] are, [as] created in the image of God" (pp. 23-24). Introspection is part of the meditative process and is a fancy word that means either "looking within one's self" or "reflecting," which comes from the Latin word *speculum* literally meaning "speculation" (Delio,

2004, p. 93). Prayerfully reflecting upon daily activities is a good practice for youth, that is, to recount all actions at the end of the day. Delio (2004) offers adolescents meditation questions to consider as they embark on their quest of becoming more spiritual. Ideally, the questions can be meditated on over the course of days and weeks.

> (1) Who is the God to whom you pray? What is your image of God? What is the gender of your God and why?
>
> (2) Where are you in your relation to God at this present time? Are you striving for a wholehearted relationship with God?
>
> (3) How does prayer influence the shape of your life? Do you view prayer as an integral part of your life? What helps you to pray? What distracts you from prayer?
>
> (4) As you pray, try to enter into your heart. What do you find? Do you pray honestly or do you wear a "mask" by presenting an image of who you think God wants to see rather than who you really are? What are some of the difficulties of honestly facing who you are?
>
> (5) Pray and reflect on the text Jeremiah 31:3: "I have loved you with an everlasting love; therefore, I have continued my faithfulness to you."
>
> (6) How do you live in relation to a God of faithful love? What do you find difficult in your relationship with God? (pp. 29, 69)

These questions may be helpful for young people as they meditate and reflect upon their faith life and relationship with

God. For Delio, the spiritual practice of meditation with teenagers has a pedagogical approach that involves reflection, introspection, and stillness, which can give young people clarity and self-awareness.

## 2. The Examen

Another good strategy that can be useful for empowering adolescents in meditation is the examination of conscience, and it is a good tool for adolescents to learn to help cultivate their spirituality. Saint Ignatius of Loyola (1491-1556), the sixteenth century Spanish mystic and founder of the Society of Jesus (Jesuits) pioneered this daily spiritual exercise that has been coined the "examination of conscience." Today, this observance is referred to as the *Examen of Consciousness* or the *Ignatian Examen*, a spiritual system of introspection, recollection, and meditation, which has a twofold purpose: (a) trying to find God in all things and (b) working to gain freedom to cooperate with God's will.

Catholic spiritual writer Phyllis Zagano (2003) reports that there are five steps that may help young Christians become more spiritually attuned to God: (a) recall you are in the presence of God, (b) look at your day with gratitude, (c) ask help from the Holy Spirit, (d) review your day, and (e) reconcile and resolve (pp. 2-4). Step four of the *Examen* is the longest part of the process, which includes asking poignant questions: When did I fail? When did I love? What were my good habits? What are my life patterns today? See both the positive and negative in life. See other forms of God's presence in the world (Zagano, pp. 3-4). The *Examen* provides adolescents with a tangible and realistic plan to review their day or their week. The main point of introspection and the *Examen* is to find the sources of un-freedom, disingenuous attitudes, self-deception in one's life-old habits, people, situations, conditions-that lead one to make "cramped" choices away from determining and discerning the will of God. Teaching adolescents to integrate introspection is a positive way that will allow them to examine their conscience and to discern their actions.

### 3. Discernment

The spiritual practice of discernment can also be a powerful ally to meditation. Boosting adolescent spirituality deserves some elements of discernment, that is, the ability to judge and estimate that which is worthy, useful, and from God and that which is peripheral, noxious, and void of God. Jesuit theologian Michael J. Buckley (1993) indicates, "All human beings who search for God want God to guide their lives, and Christians have been taught normatively to expect 'to be guided by the [Holy] Spirit' (Galatians 5:18; Romans 8:14)" (p. 274). Therefore, adolescent discernment involves a young person's conscience, character, life choices, and spiritual decisions.

Catholic theologians Lawrence S. Cunningham and Keith J. Egan (1996) observe, "Our experience must be tempered or judged with the same aids by which we form conscience: through sound teaching, through the aid of the larger community, by the tradition of the spiritual masters/mistresses of the past" (p. 20). A juvenile's faith community directly impacts personal spiritual discernment; therefore, community involvement and interaction are indispensable for seeking spiritual awareness. Guiding youth in the discernment process places great emphasis upon religious experience, conversion, and community interaction with God. Discernment is a necessary spiritual "burden" and is important in determining God's will in decisions that are distinct from human ingenuity and those spiritual forces that are lacking God's graciousness entirely.

Catholic theologian Robert Barron (2002) observes that discernment is the process of watching and listening, which entails "hunting down the will and movement of God" (p. 146). Barron describes discernment in terms of four imperatives: (a) being attentive, (b) being intelligent, (c) being reasonable, and (d) being responsible (pp. 146-151). These four imperatives are verbs that ideally call young people into action. Being attentive is to see the world non-selectively or superficially; being intelligent is about "grasping" concepts and ideas tantamount to an "ah-ha" moment; being reasonable is the hard-edged process of judgment and deciding that which is right or wrong; being responsible is the uncomfortable path of abiding in the first three imperatives and taking the appropriate action.

Methodist religious educator David F. White (2005) in a recent book *Practicing Discernment with Youth: A Transformative Youth Ministry Approach* maintains that youth ministries are poised to reclaim the Catholic practice of discernment because contemporary youth culture is in crisis. For White, crisis creates "an opportunity to relinquish our unreserved trust in contemporary culture and embody the beauty and wholeness we have glimpsed in a trustworthy God" (2005, p. 63). This opportunity is to teach youth to reclaim the spiritual practice of discernment. White classifies discernment into four areas that emphasize adolescent capacities:

> (a) discernment as a language of the *heart* that focuses on affect and intuition, through which God speaks; (b) discernment as a language of the *mind*, which engages in intellectual analysis through which God speaks; (c) discernment as language of the *soul*, which God speaks; and (d) discernment as a language of the *body*, of practical exploration of the world, through which God also speaks." (2005, pp. 66-67, italics added).

White maintains an integrated approach to practicing discernment with youth, which involves the *totus persona*-heart, mind, soul, and body-has the best chance to penetrate young people in an increasingly isolated culture. These four areas are actualized in a fourfold drama of: (a) *ortho-pathos* or listening (loving God with your heart); (b) *ortho-optomai* or understanding (loving God with your mind); (c) *ortho-doxy* or remembering/dreaming (loving God with your soul); and (d) *ortho-praxis* or acting (loving God with your strength and service), and taken together offer a transformative and alternative approach to youth ministry (White, 2005, p. 88; Illustration on Pg. 111 from same source).[22]

Finally, White (2005) states, "The healing needed among youth demands that we introduce them to the practices of discernment that engage their whole selves" (pp. 84-85). Practicing discernment with Catholic teenagers fosters Christian identity and cultivates adolescent spirituality, which will encourage exploration into their personal faith life.

Finally, I would certainly be remiss as a Catholic adolescent ministry scholar if I did not mention the 1,000-year tradition of praying the Rosary, because it is a form of meditation that is encouraged as a meditative, non-liturgical, and private prayer form by the Catholic Church (Pope Paul VI, 1974; Pope John Paul II, 1987, 2002; *Catechism of the Catholic Church*, no. 2676-2679, 2708). For the sake of those readers who are either non-Catholic, who are unfamiliar with this meditative prayer, or who are suspicious about the Rosary, I offer a few brief comments. The Rosary is a series of biblically based prayers, most of which are addressed to Mary of Nazareth to, in turn, *pray for* the petitioner who is praying the Rosary. Traditionally, these prayers have been said while counting prayer beads and it is not intended to be some magical incantation, but more of a reflection on the life of the person who is praying, and upon Mary's life as a symbol of the Church and discipleship, and on the life of Christ.

Pope John Paul II (2002) states, "The Rosary, though clearly Marian in character, is at heart a Christo-centric prayer. In the sobriety of its elements, it has all the *depth of the Gospel message in its entirety*, of which it can be said to be a compendium" (n. 1). There are four mysteries of the Rosary that are to be reflected upon by the person who is praying the Rosary. The Joyful Mysteries focus on the Annunciation, Visitation, Nativity, presentation of Jesus at the Jerusalem Temple, and finding the child Jesus in the Temple. The Luminous Mysteries focus on baptism of Jesus in the Jordan, the wedding at Cana, Jesus' first proclamation of the Kingdom of God, the Transfiguration, and the institution of Sunday Eucharist. The Sorrowful Mysteries focus on the agony in the Garden of Gethsemane, Jesus scourging at the pillar, the crowing of thorns, the carrying of the cross, and Crucifixion. The Glorious Mysteries focus on the Resurrection, the Ascension, the Descent of the Holy Spirit, the Assumption of Mary, and the heavenly Coronation of the Blessed Virgin Mary.

Praying the Rosary as a reflective discipline incorporates the mysteries of Christ's life and is relatively easy to learn. Catholic youth ministers will be able to incorporate without difficulty the Rosary as a legitimate prayer form and as a spiritual practice that can enrich Catholic spirituality in teenagers. The Rosary's ultimate purpose is to bring young Catholics closer to God through introspection and reflection upon the life of Christ. The Rosary is an excellent spiritual tool for youth ministers to integrate in a variety of youth ministry settings: at a special parish youth gathering, on retreats, at the end of study of Mary, on mission trips, at youth conference, etc. The spiritual beauty of the Rosary is that it has the ability to be integrated into just about any ministry setting.

Fortunately, for adolescents the Rosary is a structured prayer form that incorporates the mysteries of Christ's life and is relatively easy to learn. Catholic youth ministers should be able to incorporate without difficulty the Rosary as a legitimate prayer form and as a spiritual meditation practice that can enrich Catholic spirituality in teenagers. The Second Vatican Council (1963-1965) document, *Lumen Gentium* (1964) gently reminds Catholics against Marian abuse: "The Magisterium of the Church . . . exhorts theologians and preachers of the divine word to abstain zealously both from all gross exaggerations as well as from petty narrow-mindedness in considering the singular dignity of the Mother of God" (n. 67). For non-Catholics, it is important to keep an open mind about this Catholic ritual and that the Rosary's ultimate purpose is to bring Catholics closer to God through personal introspection and reflection upon the life of Christ.

Meditation with young people will be challenging because it involves the recognition of conversion, responsiveness of consciousness, discernment, and theological reflection, which may be beyond their mental and spiritual capacities without adult facilitation and supervision. Certainly meditation is not impossible, but these elements as described are characteristic of a more mature adolescent faith-life in Christ. Once an adolescent feels comfortable with five-minute, 10-minute, and 20-minute meditations, then it may be time to consider "resting in God" or "praying with the heart." Saint and Pope Gregory the Great (540-604) is attributed with saying that "praying with the heart" is tantamount to contemplative prayer. Contemplation is the next step in the meditative process and goes a bit "deeper" than does meditation.

## The Spiritual Practice of Contemplation

Contemplation is perhaps the most difficult spiritual practice for adolescents to master, but it can be accomplished. Contemplation is an experience of "being present to God" or "being caught up with God" and is much more reflective practice and discipline than meditation because it requires and entails more silence, solitude, and stillness (Canales, 2009b, p. 66). Contemplation is not simplistic or geared for all people, and youth ministers would be naïve if they did not believe that contemplation is a sophisticated and complicated process. Contemplation is a spiritual discipline that evolves and moves from self-awareness to self-acceptance to self-actualization (Canales, 2009b, p. 66).

Ilia Delio (2004) comments that Saint Francis of Assisi (1181-1224) describes contemplation as "'seeing with the eyes of the Spirit'" (p. 130). Saint Francis' understanding of contemplation is both simple and profound: simple because no one person alone possesses an esoteric or elitist experience of God (contemplation is for all mature Christians), profound because one must be imbued by the Holy Spirit before contemplation takes place. In another work, Delio (2005) affirms that contemplation is a vision or gaze between God and the Christian engaged in contemplative prayer. She writes,

> Contemplation is a penetrating gaze that gets to the heart of reality. It is looking into the depths of things with the eyes of the heart and seeing them in their true relation to God. It is a type of vision that sees things for their true worth, their individual uniqueness and distinction, the fact that each thing is singularly wanted and loved by God. (p. 132)

The message is that contemplation involves self-awareness, self-acceptance, and self-actualization, which all lead to transformation in Christ-the pinnacle expression of spirituality. Classical contemplation in the Catholic tradition is an attitude of the heart and mind that requires an interrelated worldview and finely attuned interior life, which spiritual masters or mystics such as Benedict of Nursia (480-547), Dominic of Osma (1170-1221), Meister Eckhart (1260-1328), Julia of Norwich (1342-1420), Teresa of Avila (1515-1582), John of the Cross (1542-1591), Therese of Lisieux (1873-1898), and Thomas Merton (1915-1968) acquired over decades of serious prayer, introspection, and discernment. Unfortunately, the practice of contemplation in the Catholic Church over the centuries has been utilized predominately by adults, and many of the contemplation techniques have been designed for adults. Recently, however, new research sheds some light on spiritual practice of contemplation involving adolescents.

The spiritual practice of contemplation also involves silence and solitude, which needs to be created by the person seeking contemplation. Cunningham and Egan (1996) suggest that authentic contemplation is totally *wordless, symbol-less*, and *imageless*, that is, it is totally void and passive in nature, seeking nothing and expecting nothing (pp. 99-100). The quest for contemplation is coupled with the desire for more solitude. Solitude usually nourishes and strengthens the interior life of a contemplative person. Teenagers are full of energy and enthusiasm, making contemplation demanding for them. The spiritual practice of contemplation works in the exact opposite direction of typical adolescent behavior, but it can still be accomplished with juveniles as a method of enriching spirituality.

Mark Yaconelli (2006) maintains that contemplative prayer in youth ministry is an invitation for adolescents to enter into a more meaningful relationship with the triune God. He offers two ancient Catholic prayer practices that can be adjusted to fit a youth ministry curricula: (1) *lectio divina* and (2) centering prayer. It may be quite helpful to examine each of these contemplation strategies for the purpose of enlivening adolescent spirituality.

## 1. Lectio Divina

*Lectio divina* is an invitation to reflect and read the *sacra pagina* (sacred pages), but it does not have to be exclusively Scripture: spiritual writings, patristic and medieval theological writings, and lives of the saints can also be read and reflected upon. It is important for adults who minister to and with adolescents that *lectio divina* is not tantamount to biblical exegesis, scriptural hermeneutics, and the study of the word of God for advancing theological sciences. According to Catholic liturgical scholar Kevin W. Irwin (1993), *lectio divina* has a basic twofold formula: (a) "*lectio divina* includes reading, private prayer, and

(b) *meditatio*, with 'meditation' meaning the memorization, repetition, and prayerful rumination ('chewing over') of texts as a stimulus to personal prayer" (p. 596). Along similar lines, Canales (2004b) states that *lectio divina* has a fourfold formula, "The church has developed diverse non-liturgical prayer forms since ancient times: *lectio*, reading from the Bible; *meditatio*, applying the reading to one's life; *oratio*, petitioning God for guidance, understanding, and wisdom; and *contemplatio*, contemplating the God-experience while in prayer" (p. 40). The *lectio divina* is a good pastoral vehicle to help strengthen adolescent spirituality, but the youth ministers who lead this encounter must feel confident and comfortable facilitating the experience.

Yaconelli (2006) presents a modified Catholic approach to *lectio divina* for youth ministers to integrate with their teenagers. Yaconelli admits, "The steps of this prayer might seem arbitrary and complicated at first. But as you engage in the prayer, you'll find the process is quite natural" (p. 85). There are six steps to engage Catholic young people in the *lectio divina* process.

> **Preparation.** Begin by finding a passage of scripture to pray with. You can choose a passage based on a lectionary, a daily devotional, or simply select a passage on your own. Make sure the scripture is not too long. Next, find a quiet place to pray where you won't be distracted or interrupted-a place where you feel safe and comfortable opening up to God. Often it is helpful to light a candle or set out a sacred object, something beautiful that quiets your spirit and reminds you of God's nearness.

> **Silence.** Once you've found a place to pray, take a moment merely to rest, relaxing into God's presence. With each breath become aware of God's love for you. Say a simple prayer offering yourself to God and welcoming whatever the Holy Spirit has for you.

**Reading.** Read the passage once to get oriented to the text. Then read it slowly a second time, and then again a third time, listening for a word or phrase that seems to shimmer or stand out in bold- a word that seems to address you. It may be a word that draws your attention through either attraction or repulsion.

**Meditation.** Once a word or phrase has been given, repeat it to yourself, allowing the rest of the text to fall away. As you prayerfully repeat it, different thoughts, feelings, and images may arise. Allow this word to touch all that arises-thoughts, hopes, memories, images, and feelings. What do you notice? What is being offered?

**Oration.** Let yourself express prayers of petition or gratitude as they arise. Your meditation on the word may uncover a place of pain or regret. Pray about it to God. You may notice a person or situation that needs prayer. Pray that to God, too. Honestly express your deepest thoughts, feelings, and desires in dialogue with God. Pray yourself empty.

**Contemplation.** Finally, allow yourself to simply rest in God, like a child resting in her mother's lap. Lay down all of the insights, words, and images you've encountered and simply dwell in the presence of God. Sink into God beneath all your thoughts and feelings. (pp. 85-86)

As youth ministers engage adolescents in the *lectio divina* process, they may find themselves in a place that refreshes and edifies their spirituality, and opens their mind, heart, and entire being to the presence of God.

## 2. Centering Prayer

The contemplative technique of centering prayer is yet another way that may enhance adolescent spirituality in teenagers. Yaconelli (2006) notes, "This form of prayer trusts the direct and immediate availability of God, the 'indwelling Christ,' who is nearer than our own heartbeat" (p. 87). Centering prayer is part of the contemplative process, which leads to interior transformation.

Cistercian monk Thomas Keating (1993) comments, "Centering prayer is a method designed to facilitate the development of contemplative prayer by preparing one's faculties to cooperate with this gift . . . it is not meant to replace other kinds of prayer; it simply puts other kinds of prayer into a new and fuller perspective" (p. 139). Centering prayer in many respects is a simplified version of the *lectio divina* and it is not an end in itself, but a beginning because it enjoys less "study" and "thinking" about God and concentrates on resting or relaxing and "being" in God's holy presence (Yaconelli, 2006, p. 87; Keating, 1993, p. 139).

Yaconelli (2006) provides a revised Catholic model for *centering prayer*, which he gleans from Keating, for youth ministers to integrate with their teenagers. Yaconelli states, "Centering prayer is a direct, immediate, and deceptively simple form of silent prayer" (p. 88). There are five steps to engage Catholic young people in the centering prayer method.

> **Sit.** Sit comfortably in a space where you can open yourself to God. Have a set time to pray-10 minutes or so is good for starters. You may want to light a candle to help remind you of God's nearness.
>
> **Select.** Before you begin the prayer, choose a sacred word as the symbol of your intention to be with God. This word expresses your desire to be in God's presence and to yield to the movement of the Holy Spirit. Ask the Holy Spirit to reveal a

word that is suitable for you. Examples include *Jesus, Lord, Abba, Love, Mercy, Stillness, Faith, Trust, Shalom,* and *Amen*. Once you've selected a word, stick with it. Occasionally, people get caught up worrying whether their word feels right for them, wondering about the various meanings of their word, comparing their word to other words, or wondering if some other word might be more "spiritual" and produce "better" results. Do not take your word so seriously. It's simply a reminder of your desire to be with God. What's significant in this prayer is your intention (to be with God), and not your particular word.

**Welcome.** Before you pray, close your eyes and settle yourself. Allow a spirit of rest and hospitality to come over your body. Welcome God into this time. Briefly and silently introduce your sacred word as the symbol of your consent to God's presence and action within and around you. Thomas Keating suggests introducing the sacred word "inwardly and as laying a feather on a piece of cotton."

**Be aware.** As you pray, you will become aware of thoughts, memories, commentaries, and images. When you notice your mind wandering, gently return to the sacred word. Thoughts are a normal part of centering prayer; yet by quietly returning to the sacred word, minimal effort is used to bring attention back to God.

**Silence.** At the end of the prayer period, remain in silence with your eyes closed for a minute or two. You may want to close with the "Our Father" (Lord's Prayer) or some other formal prayer as a way of drawing the prayer to a close. (pp. 88-89; bold words added by this author)

When teaching youth to engage in centering prayer, the most obvious obstacle will be the quieting of the "chattering mind," but this can be overcome with patience and practice. As Delio (2004) reminds us, the goal of centering prayer is imitation of Christ, and not necessarily union with God (although that is very important); imitation leads to interior transformation (p. 68).

Other typical contemplation techniques that youth ministers may implement with Catholic teenagers are: (1) concentrating on the importance of celebrating Eucharist (Sunday Mass) while contemplating the Scripture pericopes for that particular Sunday, and (2) experiencing forms of Eucharistic worship apart from the Sunday assembly known as Eucharistic Exposition and Benediction[23] ("adoration" as most youth ministers refer to it, and as explained in chapter 3), which may engage a juvenile in prayer while sitting in front of the Blessed Sacrament[24] (Canales, 2009a, pp. 11-15). Whichever contemplative prayer experience is selected by a youth minister to implement in youth ministry, the Catholic youth contemplation methods need to support spirituality and life themes that will help to magnetize adolescents' interest in bolstering their spirituality (Crawford & Rossiter, 1996, p. 134).

## The Practice of Spiritual Direction

Spiritual direction is an age-old practice that has taken place between pupils and spiritual guides who practice the art of listening. Jesuit priests and noted spiritual directors William A. Barry and William J. Connolly (1978) state, "Spiritual direction puts primary focus on experience of God, most often occurring in prayer. . . therefore, religious experience is to spiritual direction what food is to cooking. Without religious experience there can be no spiritual direction" (p. 8). The spiritual director of the adolescent must empower the young person to focus on their relationship and encounters with God. The pinnacle purpose of spiritual direction with teenagers is to guide youth toward continual conversion leading to spiritual regeneration and transformation. The method by which spiritual direction takes place is listening or active listening.

The whole process is a spiritualization and interiorization that takes place within a person's life. Spiritual direction with a teenager is a process that affects the spiritual life and interior life of a young person; thus, the spiritualization is accomplished by way of interiorization and introspection; however, our interior life is closely connected with our exterior actions and attitudes. Monastic spiritual directors Francis K. Nemeck and Marie T. Coombs (1993) state,

> Spiritual direction deals with the interior life of the directees: their life in God, and their life with all creation. Spiritual direction addresses the process on interiorization in such a way as to awaken directees to a consciousness of the path along which God is leading them. They in turn can then more voluntarily cooperate with God as [God] draws them through the passages of life. (p. 32)

The practice of spiritual direction is a wonderful pastoral tool to help a young person to better achieve spiritual awareness and to deepen their prayer and faith life, but the responsibility still rests on the adolescent who desires to become closer to God.

Current research on Christian spiritual direction suggests that today's spiritual director who works with juveniles is more of a spiritual guide allowing the Holy Spirit to take the lead in facilitating the direction process. Catholic spiritual director Carolyn Gratton (1993) explains, "Realizing that neither therapeutic counseling nor classic prayer-guidance is sufficient in itself, today's directors are opting for a more foundational approach that, while incorporating one faith tradition as ultimate, has links to other cultures and traditions as well" (p. 915). Catholic spiritual direction with teenagers is concerned with "being in touch" with the pneumatic characteristics that are in the heart, mind, soul, and body of the young person who seeks spiritual guidance.

Youth ministry educator Dori G. Baker (2005) indicates that the art of holy listening can enrich the faith lives of teenagers and is an urgent task for contemporary youth ministry (p. 53). For Baker, holy listening and evoking youth testimonies through holy listening is likened to spiritual direction with adolescents. Baker observes, "In the presence of an artful listener, a youth may better be able to discern a pattern of calling, claiming, and ongoing revelation woven through these life events" (p. 54). Questions that adolescent ethnographic listeners and/or spiritual directors might ask while trying to evoke youth testimony may include:

> 1. How would you describe the family, church, and community in which you were formed?
>
> 2. What kind of ideas or experiences have you had as a young person that have destabilized or called into question your early faith?
>
> 3. What resources, rituals, practices, or ideas are you finding helpful as you look to your faith to guide you in life?

These questions coupled with a patient youth minister or adult youth leader can foster an ethos of holy listening and can be a valuable pastoral approach to improve the adolescent-adult relationship in the youth ministry and to increase adolescent spirituality. One of the main pastoral dilemmas surrounding spiritual direction and holy listening are finding qualified and competently trained adults to facilitate such spiritual companionship with adolescents

### *The Crux of the Issue: Finding Trained Adult Youth Leaders*

The real issue is the lack of trained youth ministers and adult youth leaders to do the work of spiritual direction in the Catholic Church. The question is not *why* spiritual direction with teenagers, but *how*. Yaconelli (2005) notes, "How do you help [youth ministers] become not just 'religious educators,' but 'spiritual guides'-people who know how to tend the spiritual hunger within [young people]" (p. 39)? The crux of the matter is that most Catholic youth ministers are not properly trained in spiritual direction. A fair question to ask is: How many are qualified to do this type of spiritual and introspective work with teenagers? What are the prospects for training youth ministers to be spiritual directors? Far and few between! The overwhelming majority of youth ministers that I know simply are not qualified to do this type of spiritual and introspective work with teenagers.

As cited earlier in the book, Orthodox bishop Joseph F. Purpura (2008) maintains that one of the greatest needs in the young church is attaining proper and professional spiritual direction. Consequently, then, spiritual direction is not being offered to the young church because there is a real lack of qualified adult spiritual directors who focus their ministry spiritual direction with teenagers. As young people seek to deepen their understanding of the Church, their spiritual lives, and their relationship with God, it is thwarted by the great lack of spiritual direction available to them (Purpura, p. 1). This statement sounds all too familiar in the Catholic Church and is a real dichotomy in Catholic youth ministry. Catholic teenagers need and deserve spiritual direction, but "there appears to be no great commitment or effort towards providing spiritual direction to our young people, and despite this, our young people on their own continue to seek such direction" (Purpura, p. 2).

The concern is the way in which youth ministers and adult youth leaders who work with Catholic teenagers may contribute to their spiritual formation with little or no training in such spiritual methods. Crawford and Rossiter (2004) maintain that the role of religious education, spiritual formation, and spiritual direction are rudimentary goals of youth ministry education (p. 71). Therefore, it seems logical that Catholic colleges that offer degrees or certificates in youth ministry studies and youth ministry educators may want to provide courses and classes on spiritual direction for teenagers or adolescent spiritual direction.

A real example of the "crisis" that Purpura writes is the fact that in the Roman Catholic Diocese of Austin, Texas—where I used to live and work—there are 125 parishes spanning 22,000 square miles (roughly the same size as the state of West Virginia). Of those 125 churches, there are 100 youth ministers under my former pastoral care and guidance, and there are only three to five youth ministers who are capable of spiritual direction with young people; that is, there are only three to five youth ministers who have gone through the formal training that allows them to function as professionally trained spiritual directors. However, these few youth ministers are not engaged in the ongoing practice of adolescent spiritual direction because of time constraints. Moreover, the Diocese of Austin has an Institute for Spiritual Direction, which has a three-year program to train adults to become certified spiritual directors. Many of the 195 Catholic dioceses in the United States are following Austin with similar certificate programs in spiritual direction. Clearly, in the Diocese of Austin, many are called to youth ministry, but few are called to the practice of spiritual direction. The distinction between spiritual direction and pastoral advice is important in the Catholic Church. Authentic spiritual direction must be performed by a trained and *certified* spiritual director holding certain qualifications demonstrating that the person has been professionally trained and has had proper hours of supervision, much like a licensed counselor. In reality, whether certified or not, Catholic youth ministers accompany young people on their spiritual journey, by allowing them to share their stories (White, 2005), engaging in holy listening (Baker, 2005), providing mentorship (Purpura 2008), and becoming connected with them (Yaconelli, 2005), all as part of the intimate relationship between adolescent directee and adult director.

## The Skill Set Needed to be an Effective Spiritual Director to Adolescents

There are specific skill sets that adolescent spiritual directors need. Catholic youth specialist Gregory Rohde (1991) comments on the attributes, knowledge, and skill set that a spiritual director with adolescents should possess. A successful spiritual director of adolescents must:

(1) be a person of prayer

(2) know about articulating faith encounters and life experiences

(3) be called to be a continual student

(4) be familiar with the dynamics of healthy relationships

(5) be acutely aware of the danger of falling in love with the directee

(6) be versed in spiritual growth-conversion, struggle, and integration

(7) be able to support and challenge the directee at appropriate times

(8) be a person of integrity, ethics, and authenticity possess a spirit of hospitality and availability

(9) be characterized by vulnerability and humility possess the gifts of wisdom, discipline, and detachment

(10) have a genuine love for teenagers

(11) have a respect for the capabilities of young people,

(12) guard against spiritual fatigue or burnout

(13) possess a sense of humor and spirit of hope (pp. 178-180)

It is easy to see that a spiritual director for adolescents must be capable of a wide range of spiritual functions. Although many youth ministers possess these abilities, that alone does not qualify them as spiritual directors in the Catholic Church. Spiritual direction with adolescents involves and implies pastoral advice, but offering pastoral advice is in no way tantamount to spiritual direction, at least in the Catholic worldview.

Catholic congregations must be willing to invest the time, financial resources, and energy to help develop the skill set required to do spiritual direction with young people. Yaconelli (2005) states, "A youth ministry begins with adults" (p. 123). Therefore, in order for spiritual direction to flourish in the youth community, there must be an outgrowth of adult responsibility and accountability. Catholic adolescent ministry specialist Thomas East (2004) notes that adult youth leaders must be properly trained, "Adult leaders need to grow in their faith and learn skills for ministry; it is important to match the gifts and talents of adult leaders to the right roles in the youth ministry" (p. 67). Effective parishes do not assume that adults automatically will be good at working with youth. Adults must learn the skill set necessary to become competent youth workers, mentors, and spiritual directors, but most of all they must respect and have a heart for working with teenagers (East, pp. 64-67).

Finally, spiritual direction with adolescents is an exercise in trust on the part of the juvenile and an exercise of patience and compassion on the part of the adult. As previously mentioned by Clement Mehlman (2000) spiritual direction with adolescents is "sometimes a-floatin and sometimes go a-fishin" (p. 1-2). The key to spiritual direction with young people is being a good listener, being non-judgmental, and accepting them where they are in their lives. Spiritual direction with youth is both intriguing and entertaining as you help to empower them to on their journey with God and self. Together-adult spiritual director and youth directee-fashion a relationship that weaves a spiritual and faith tapestry that deepens the bond between God and adolescent and further cultivates teenage spirituality.

## Summary

The three spiritual disciplines of meditation, contemplation, and spiritual direction are wonderful spiritual practices for adults to integrate into their lives and ministries, and should not be overlooked for cultivating adolescents in their quest for spiritual development. Crawford and Rossiter (1996, 2004) argue that with so many youth joining spiritual movements such as sects and cults and being heavily influenced by music, film, television, video games, and the Internet, it is no wonder that fostering Christian spirituality, religious identity, and moral development is important to those who evaluate youth and educate those who work with youth (1996, p. 138; 2004, p. 69). The NFCYM (1986) document, *The Challenge of Adolescent Catechesis: Maturing in Faith* observes, "We cannot expect more of youth than we do of adults. The ways we adults learn about, express, and live out faith is a vigorous support or a serious obstacle in effectively catechizing youth" (p. 60).

Many adults in our society are not very good at meditation, contemplation, or spiritual direction, so these spiritual practices may be challenging for adolescents, but doing theology and ministry with youth is demanding work that needs to be taken seriously. As illustrated in this essay, meditation, contemplation, and spiritual direction can be achieved by adolescents. There are pastoral strategies that can be implemented by Catholic youth ministers to strengthen adolescent spirituality. There has been a recent resurgence in the youth ministry arena to help enhance Christian adolescent spirituality in Catholic teenagers (Canales, 2009a/b; Crawford & Rossier, 2004; Delio, 2004, 2005; Engbretson, 2006; Mehlmann, 2000; Tacey, 2004; White, 2005, 2008; Wright 2000; Yaconelli, 2005, 2006; Zagano, 2003).

These three spiritual practices are part of the "spiritual revolution" taking place among Catholic adolescents who "do not fit the Church mold" and who seem to show "disaffection towards religion," and who are seeking a "spiritual experience" or "spiritual awakening" (McQuillan, 2004, pp. 8-9). The findings from White and Yaconelli indicate adolescents prefer an experiential type of spirituality and desire a living spirituality that interacts and connects with their young lives. Meditation, contemplation, and spiritual direction fit the adolescent's need for experiential spirituality. Tacey (2004) believes so strongly in the way that experience influences spirituality in juveniles that he makes an appeal that the triad of Catholic education, Scripture, tradition, and history be expanded to include experience because God is not dead, God is dynamic, and God is experiential. Hence, spirituality should be dynamic and experiential for young people (pp. 92-105). Tacey (2004) and McQuillan (2004) maintain that adolescent spirituality is alive and well in Catholic youth, but there needs to be a rejuvenation of traditional methods that are life-giving and promote energetic faith in teenagers.

## Discussion Questions

(1) As a young person, did you ever experience any of the three spiritual practices mentioned in this chapter-meditation, contemplation, and spiritual direction? If so, how? If not, why?

(2) Which of these three spiritual practices-meditation, contemplation, and spiritual direction-would appear difficult for the teenagers you know to integrate into their lives? Explain your rationale.

(3) Review the meditation section of the chapter. Which of the three areas seem to resonate best with you and the youth of your parish: Introspection, the Examen, or Discernment?

(4) Review the contemplation section of the chapter. Which of the two areas seem to resonate best with you and the youth of your parish: *lectio divina* or centering prayer?

(5) Do you think there is a real need for spiritual direction with adolescents? Is spiritual direction provided to the adolescents in your parish? Does the person have a degree, certificate, or license to practice spiritual direction? Do you feel such credentials are necessary to offer spiritual direction to adolescents?

A Noble Quest

CHAPTER SIX

# STRENGTHS AND LIMITATIONS OF THE PASTORAL PRACTICE OF CULTIVATING ADOLESCENT SPIRITUALITY IN CATHOLIC YOUTH MINISTRY SETTINGS

*"Being young today means having to face many problems due to unemployment and the lack of clear ideas and real possibilities for the future. At times you can have the impression of being powerless in the face of current crises and their repercussions. Despite these difficulties, do not let yourselves be discouraged, and do not give up on your dreams! Instead, cultivate all the more your heart's great desire for fellowship, justice, and peace. The future is in the hands of those who know how to seek and find sound reasons for life and hope."*[25]

**Pope Benedict XVI**
*25th Anniversary of the
Inauguration of World Youth Day 2010*

This short chapter is important because it highlights six strengths and four limitations that should be helpful for youth ministers who want to make cultivating adolescent spirituality one of the primary foci of their ministry. Although there have been three spiritual practices identified that are appropriate for high school age adolescents, there are many others that can be fruitfully employed in youth ministry. Choosing spiritual practices and on deciding their overall place in the scope of Catholic youth ministry can be difficult; therefore, it is important to analyze the strengths and limitations of this approach and its application to adolescents.

## The Strengths of Focusing Youth Ministry on the Cultivation of Adolescent Spirituality

There are several significant strengths in cultivating adolescent spirituality in Christian teenagers that make it attractive to youth ministry. The first advantage of cultivating adolescent spirituality in youth is that it attempts to empower teenagers with a deeper spirituality that integrates the transcendent and tries to stimulate the sacred within their lives. The process of becoming a more spiritually attuned adolescent can be achieved through self-awareness and personal discovery, but like anything worthwhile, there is a personal sacrifice involved (Canales, 2004b, p. 48). In the midst of the process of developing spiritually, teenagers may find themselves moving into a more meaningful relationship with Jesus Christ and may also find beauty and solace in the Church in which they profess their faith.

A second positive feature of cultivating spirituality in adolescents is that teenagers are able to experience various spiritual programs and initiatives that youth ministries provide, such as diverse prayer experiences, inspirational worship, weekend retreats, youth conferences, and extended trips. According to RTV (1997), "If we are to succeed, we must offer young people a *spiritually challenging* and *world-shaping vision* that meets their hunger for the chance to *participate* in a worthy adventure" (p. 10). This is the beauty of integrating adolescent spirituality as a predominate approach for youth ministry: It allows youth ministers to design a curriculum that is heavily influenced by those tangible activities that teenagers enjoy best-hands-on experiences (Canales, 2005b, pp. 72-73). Emphasizing prayer empowers youth to understand the natural, supernatural, and metaphysical dimensions of the power of prayer. Highlighting inspirational worship connects faith-seekers of every denomination with contemporary Christian liturgy and music, with special emphasis on spiritual lyrics, upbeat tempo, and non-traditional hymns.

Focusing on weekend retreats reaches teenagers on five levels: intellectual, emotional, relational, religious, and spiritual, because weekend retreats emphasize total transformation (Canales, 2002, p. 31). Concentrating on extended trips such as participating in youth conferences, work camps, and mission trips equips young people with a rich spectrum of spiritual activities. Comprehensive youth ministry should strive to strike a balance of programs, activities, and strategies. As RTV (1997) observes, "This balance can be achieved throughout a year or a season of programming. Even a single program or strategy can incorporate several of the ministry components, as in the case of a retreat" (p. 26). These hands-on components function as the foundation; without them, a youth ministry may not become spiritually vibrant.

A third benefit is the possibility of broadening young people's spiritual horizons. Youth ministers can draw upon a variety of spiritualities and spiritual disciplines from within their own traditions, and even at times, from within other Christian traditions or world religions. Young people can begin to appreciate the richness that the Christian heritage affords them in terms of prayer and spiritual activities such as retreats, Taizé worship, journaling, *lectio divina*, Eucharistic adoration, and Bible studies.

Adolescent spirituality will be enriched as teenagers are exposed to various types of spiritualities and as they actively participate in cultivating their own spirituality (Canales, 2006, p. 223). It is a tremendous benefit for a young person to be introduced to a new spiritual idea and learn about the key concepts of that particular spirituality, and an even greater benefit to actively participate in experiencing that "flavor" of spirituality directly.

A fourth gain is that young people and adult youth leaders can cultivate their spirituality together in a friendly and non-threatening manner, which helps to create Christian disciples and servant-leaders (Canales, 2006, p. 223). Youth ministries should be concerned with the spirituality of those adults who minister to teenagers. Adolescents are typically looking for adults who are role models and exhibit a real faith life and lived compassion toward others. Youth ministers should see part of their role as developing Christian spirituality in adolescents primarily, and in adults secondarily. Catholic youth ministry is at its best when all the participants within the youth ministry deepen their Christian spirituality and mature as Christian disciples together.

A fifth merit of developing adolescent spirituality is that there will be moments and periods of silence, stillness, and solitude in our youth ministries across the country. Adolescents deserve at least a few minutes of quiet time each week at a minimum, if not each day. Quiet time is not tantamount to a "time out" administered by parents to naughty children, it is a time to calm "the monkey on our backs" and to begin to surrender to God all thoughts, anxieties, worries, pains, hopes, dreams, and frustrations. Adolescents need to take time to S.T.O.P., that is, stop all the busyness in their lives, think about their lives and their God, recognize there are options in their lives that can be investigated, and pick an alternative behavior or way of doing something.

S.T.O.P. is simply a method that I have used with adolescents for over twenty years in an attempt to begin to help them become introspective and to reflect critically. It is a rudimentary spiritual exercise and in no way is it meant to be equivalent to meditation or contemplation. It is a pastoral tool for guiding teenagers in silence. Although the deeper levels of meditation and contemplation are within the capacities of adolescents

(Tacey, 2004; White, 2005; Yaconelli, 2005, 2006), young people will always benefit from a little silence, stillness, and solitude in their lives (Cunningham & Egan, 1996).

A sixth strength of enhancing adolescent spirituality is engaging in prayer and spiritual exercises, which ideally lead to authentic Christian outreach and service (Canales, 2004a, p. C-1; Shelton, 1983, pp. 121-124). Perhaps after discovering spirituality, an adolescent will find meaning and purpose in Christian service and social justice, and will recognize that these, too, are aspects of spirituality. One strategy to instill spirituality and social justice could be to organize a march and call it "Prayer in Motion Day."

The purpose of the march could be to unite students with a particular cause, such as marching for the homeless or marching for a cure for AIDS. A typical Prayer in Motion day is focused on a particular cause that is important to a specific community. Another strategy to increase spirituality and service could be called the "24-Hour Famine," which could really unite the youth ministry around a central theme such as solidarity with the poor and the world's hungry. The 24-Hour Famine could be an overnight experience, typically called a "lock-in," but in reality, students would be serving off-site of the parish grounds. Youth ministers could organize a few events over the 24-hour period to help crystallize the focus on the hungry and homeless populations.

The importance of cultivating adolescent spirituality within the lives of young people cannot be overstated. Spiritual development will help young people as they mature into young adults and enter into full adulthood. Enhancing adolescent spirituality celebrates and deepens youth's relationship with God and develops a teenager's faith, as well as their moral and spiritual life, not only individually, but also as a member of a faith community. Conversely, no one youth ministry approach can satisfy the adolescent needs of the entire Christian community, and no one model is above criticism. Therefore, it is wise to address the shortcomings of this approach to youth ministry.

## The Limitations of Focusing Youth Ministry on the Cultivation of Adolescent Spirituality

The first limitation of trying to develop adolescent spirituality as the prevailing approach to youth ministry is that it is difficult to foster and assess a young person's spiritual development. Of course, this also holds true for trying to measure young adult and adult spiritual growth. Developing adolescent spirituality sounds like a great idea, but the reality is that many adolescents today experience prayer and worship as pale, bland, anemic, and lacking in, as the great Lutheran theologian Paul Tillich (1886-1965) called it, the "ecstatic moment" (Canales, 2006, p. 224).

For many young people, the prayer of Saint Augustine, stating, "Oh! That God would enter into my heart and inebriate it," is wishful thinking because their experience of the transcendent is not spiritual in nature. Developing adolescent spirituality must be integrated prudently and judiciously with much pastoral care to allow young people the opportunity to grow and flourish. Assessing adolescent spiritual growth is perhaps lacking because there are not sufficient pastoral tools to evaluate and critique a young person's spirituality on the parish level or within the capabilities of the youth minister. At present, the best the Catholic Church can provide is only pithy questionnaires and lengthy surveys (McQuillan, 2009).

A second concern is that unless a youth minister has a good understanding of Christian spirituality that will enhance their ministry it could be difficult to integrate some of the spiritual practices contained in this book without the youth minister having personal spiritual awareness. If a person wants to go rock climbing, then a person does not ask a base jumper or a bungee jumper to lead the expedition. The rock-climbing instructor must know about crag safety, knot-tying techniques, climbing protection, climbing harnesses, and carabineers. People are incapable of taking others where they have not yet been themselves!

Therefore, if a youth minister has little or no peak religious experience directly stemming from spiritual practices such as retreats, meditation, contemplation, or spiritual direction, then the youth minister may find it challenging and difficult to direct and empower spiritual awareness in adolescents (Canales, 2006, p. 224). Of course, this does not mean that a youth minister cannot learn to become more spiritually attuned. As salvation history has indicated, the overwhelming majority of Christian spiritual masters had to learn and work extremely hard at crafting their spirituality. Albeit a bit flippant, and despite God's grace in every individual, spirituality within people is "made, not born;" that is, spirituality must be cultivated, nourished, and sustained, if it is going to grow, blossom, and be fruitful.

A third weakness is the lack of time. Perhaps more of a significant challenge is the legitimate limitation of the usage of time in a young person's life. Developing a keener spirituality and becoming more spiritually attuned means that young people will eventually have to take personal ownership of their own spirituality and its direction, which will take time.

This may appear like a disheartening task because it requires much diligence and dedication because the majority of adolescents are already bombarded with time restraints and extra demands. Catholic teenagers yearning to cultivate a stronger spirituality will have to balance time constraints with their activities, school work, relationships, part-time jobs, and spirituality, and therefore, the lack of time can become a negative factor for adolescents encountering the Sacred (Canales, 2009b, p. 74). Catholic religious educator Michael Carotta (2002) notes, "Adolescents are also dealing with the currency of time. Both females and males are investing more of their time than ever in sports, fine arts, work, and social activities" (p. 30).

It may be quite unrealistic to place so much emphasis on becoming spiritually authentic and spiritually mature when the lives of teenagers are already so busy-school and sports may be all that most teenagers can handle. Developing a strong spiritual life, creating and logging entries into a spiritual journal, and practicing introspection and prayer techniques may add to the storm and stress of adolescence instead of having the desired opposite effect. Thus, teenagers may have a difficult time maintaining their spirituality outside of the youth ministry setting.

A fourth disadvantage is that youth ministers who focus too narrowly on adolescent spirituality by only integrating spiritual activities, exercises, and strategies will eventually have to grapple with the fact that their ministry may not be authentically comprehensive. Let me explain my seemingly crass and laconic remark. The phrase *focus too narrowly on adolescent spirituality* is a bit of a misnomer and is used to express the possible pitfalls that might occur in Catholic youth ministries that are overly assertive in one area while being pastorally shortsighted in other areas of youth ministry. On the one hand, the intent is not to offer a limiting view of Christian adolescent spirituality. On the other hand, the recovering of spiritual practices and the emphasis on spiritual formation lead not only to a deeper prayer life, but also service to the world.

This is an enormous benefit to and contribution of comprehensive Catholic youth ministry. The overarching idea here is that comprehensive youth ministry must be balanced, and ideally there should be a symbiotic association and interrelationship between the three goals, seven themes, and eight components of Catholic youth ministry as stipulated in RTV. The U.S. Catholic Bishops (1997) clearly point out that there are eight comprehensive components of youth ministry, which respond to the pastoral and catechetical needs and issues of young people. RTV (1997) states, "A comprehensive ministry with adolescents provides balance among all eight components. This balance can be achieved throughout a year or a season of programming. Even a single program or strategy can incorporate several of the ministry components, as in the case of a retreat program" (p. 26).

Therefore, a youth ministry that predominately focuses on increasing adolescent spirituality may benefit from refocusing in a direction that is more holistic in scope and purpose, and encourages and incorporates all eight comprehensive components-advocacy, catechesis, community life, evangelization, justice and service, leadership development, pastoral care, and prayer and worship.

Concentrating on the cultivation of adolescent spirituality for youth ministry can be a useful pastoral methodological approach because teenage spirituality affords youth ministers legitimate strengths that will help increase spirituality in young people. The advantages far outweigh the disadvantages in terms of molding young people into more spiritually attuned Christians who are interested in deepening their spirituality.

## Summary

This discussion of strengthening adolescent spirituality in the context of comprehensive Catholic youth ministry is meant to encourage Catholic youth ministers, and all youth ministers from every denomination for that matter, to continue to address the spiritual needs of young people. Dori Baker (2005) notes that the purpose of cultivating adolescent spirituality is to empower adolescents to discern two implicit assumptions of Christianity: (1) that one's life is intended to have purpose beyond self-fulfillment and material gain; and (2) that someone stands at the ready to help one discover that purpose-the parish youth minister (p. 65). Perhaps not every Christian would agree with these two assumptions, and indeed, there may be more assumptions that adolescent ministry scholars have regarding fostering teenage spirituality, but these are surely two that I tend to foster in my two children as they embark upon adolescence.

As I previously wrote, "Continual transformation is the ultimate goal of cultivating Christian spirituality in adolescents" (Canales, 2009b, p. 75). Strengthening Christian spirituality in Catholic adolescents is concerned with cultivating the natural aspirations for the infinite and creating a natural desire for eternal happiness because human beings are oriented toward God (Rahner, 1978, p. 53). Spiritual transformation is the pinnacle expression of becoming holy, and spiritual transformation should be the aim of adolescent spirituality and a primary goal of all youth ministry, whether Orthodox, Catholic, Protestant, or Evangelical. Teenagers will learn best through religious experiences (Baker, 2005; Canales, 2005b; Canales 2009a/b; Engebretson, 2006; McQuillian, 2004; White, 2005; Wright, 2000; Yaconelli, 2005). Therefore, creating spiritual experiences for young people to encounter God and community or to encounter God through community is perhaps the best avenue for teaching, learning, and experiencing the transcendent. "Youth do not simply want to learn about God . . . youth want to feel God, experience God's love, and enter into God's presence" (Canales, 2005b, p. 73). In this way, adolescent spiritual transformation will be reached through cultivating spirituality in teenagers.

## Discussion Questions

(1) What is your understanding of phrase *comprehensive Catholic youth ministry*? Does cultivating adolescent spirituality fit into your understanding of comprehensive Catholic youth ministry?

(2) Which one the six strengths in this chapter did you find most helpful for understanding the process of cultivating adolescent spirituality?

(3) Which one the four limitations in this chapter did you agree with or disagree with concerning adolescent spirituality?

(4) Do you feel that your parish suffers from "pastoral nearsightedness" regarding cultivating adolescent spirituality into youth ministry? In other words, are we as a Church suffering from "benign whateverism" concerning our youth's spiritual development?

(5) What would you like to see happen in the Catholic Church in the United States regarding youth ministry and cultivating adolescent spirituality in Catholic adolescents?

# A Noble Quest

# Conclusion

*"Young people are a great force in society and for evangelization . . . The particular Churches throughout the continent are clearly making real efforts to catechize young people before Confirmation and to offer them other kinds of support in developing their relationship with Christ . . . The formation process for young people must be constant and active, capable of helping them to find their place in the Church and in the world. Consequently, youth ministry must be one of the primary concerns of pastors and communities."*[26]

**Pope John Paul II**
*25th Anniversary of the*
*1999, The Church In America*

I have titled this book ***A Noble Quest*** because I firmly believe that youth ministry is the most exciting and challenging ministry in the Catholic Church today. Indeed, cultivating adolescent spirituality-arguably-is the most daunting, significant, and humbling task that youth ministers are charged with. The strengthening of spirituality in teenagers and the spiritual care of young people is the most essential mission that a parish youth minister or high school campus minister embraces-and thus, a noble quest.

Cultivating one's own spirituality is difficult enough, but trying to enhance or increase another person's spirituality can be a daunting task. Nevertheless, as Catholics, we are called to catechize our sisters and brothers in the faith and help them to grow in holiness. As Pope John Paul II (1999) suggests in the quote above, youth ministry needs to be a primary concern for the Catholic Church in the United States. Parents, pastors, and directors of religious education cannot simply assume that adolescents will become spiritual. The spirituality of adolescents needs to be cultivated by adults who are willing to risk reaching out to youth and teaching them and showing them the ways to become spiritually strong.

It baffles the mind that in 2010 that the majority of our Catholic parishes still lack a full-time youth minister. It is also disheartening to see so many diocesan youth offices combine youth, young adult, and campus ministries into one office instead of having three separate offices staffed with three different people. Not too long ago at a national youth gathering, I heard a youth ministry colleague of mine use the phrase "benign whateverism" to describe the Catholic apathy regarding youth ministry in some dioceses and parishes around the country. Catholic youth ministry is not meant to be a pastoral suggestion for young people, but a living, vibrant, and energetic Catholic reality that leads young people to experience the risen Christ in their lives, to develop their Catholic identity, and to cultivate their Catholic spirituality through activities, programs, and events that are encouraging, empowering, and age-appropriate.

Hopefully this book has been an encouragement to those who work with adolescents and an invitation to help cultivate a deeper and more meaningful spirituality in their young lives. In addition, my hope is that this book can be a pastoral and spiritual resource for parish youth ministers, diocesan directors of youth ministry, directors of religious education, priests, and bishops. My sincere hope is that this book will inspire youth ministers to risk leading young people to new levels of spiritual awareness and lead them to experience a more profound and prolific spirituality. Pope John Paul II (1999) reminds us that "Spirituality is life in Christ and [life] in the Spirit, which is accepted in faith, expressed in love, and inspired by hope, and so becomes the daily life . . ." (p. 48, n. 29). In my opinion, as I travel across the United States and I speak with diocesan directors and youth ministers about adolescent issues, cultivating adolescent spirituality is one of the highest priorities in youth ministry, but one that takes a backseat to sacramental preparation, theology of the body, and various youth-appealing "hot topics." Although those topics are paramount, there should be some integration of those topics and cultivating adolescent spirituality simultaneously. Adolescent catechesis and cultivating adolescent spirituality are not mutually exclusive; on the contrary, they need to be integrated more fully.

This book is an attempt to do my part to address the issue of adolescent spirituality and to offer practical solutions and pastoral strategies to help those engaged in Catholic youth ministry be more fully equipped in their unique and important ministry role. Catholic youth ministry-whether parish youth ministry or campus youth ministry-are significant ministry positions in the Catholic Church that require competent, professional, and empowering adults who are willing to lead the young Church today to become the spiritual leaders of the world tomorrow. American Catholic young people deserve to be spiritually attuned to God and quality compressive youth ministry that instills the mind, enlivens the spirit, and refreshes the soul is perhaps the best way to enrich and awaken the spiritual potential of inside adolescents. Ah. . . and to witness this type of transformation in young people is *truly a noble quest indeed!*

# BIBLIOGRAPHY

**Articles**

Abbott-Chapman, Joan and Denholm, Carey. (2001). "Adolescents' Risk Activities, Risk Hierarchies, and the Influence of Religiosity," *Journal of Youth Studies*, 4 (3), 279-297.

Baker, Doris G. (2005). "Evoking Testimony through Holy Listening: The Art of Interview as a Practice in Youth Ministry," *Journal of Youth and Theology*, 4 (2), 53-68.

Canales, Arthur David. (2002). "The Spiritual Significance of the Nicodemus Narrative to Youth Ministry," *The Living Light*, 38 (3), 23-32.

Canales, Arthur David. (2004a). "Spirituality: Ways to Express Belief," *Herald Times Reporter*, Manitowoc, Wisconsin (Saturday, March 27) C-1.

Canales, Arthur David. (2004b). "Integrating Christian Discipleship IS Franciscanism," *Journal of the Association of Franciscan Colleges and Universities*, 1 (1), 34-53.

Canales, Arthur David. (2005a). "A Reality Check: Addressing Catholic Hispanic Youth Ministry in the United States of America (Part 1)," *Apuntes: Reflexíones Teológicas desde el Contexto Hispano-Latino*, 25 (1), 4-23.

Canales, Arthur David. (2005b). "Reaping What We Sow: Addressing Catholic Hispanic Youth Ministry in the United States of America (Part 2)," *Apuntes: Reflexíones Teológicas desde el Contexto Hispano-Latino*, 25 (2), 44-74.

Canales, Arthur David. (2006). "Models for Adolescent Ministry: Exploring Eight Ecumenical Examples," *Religious Education*, 101 (2), 204-232.

Canales, Arthur David. (2007). "The Ten-Year Anniversary of *Renewing the Vision*: Reflection on Its Impact for Catholic Youth Ministry," *New Theology Review*, 20 (2), 58-69.

# Bibliography

Canales, Arthur David. (2009a). "Strengthening Eucharistic Spirituality in Adolescents," *Emmanuel: Eucharistic Spirituality*, 115 (1), 9-23.

Canales, Arthur David. (2009b). "A Noble Quest: Cultivating Christian Spirituality in Catholic Adolescents and the Usefulness of 12 Pastoral Practices," *International Journal of Children's Spirituality*, 14 (1), 63-77.

Canales, Arthur David. (2010a). "Addressing Catholic Adolescent Spirituality and Assessing Three Spiritual Practices for Young People in Catholic Youth Ministry," *The Journal of Youth Ministry*, 8 (2), 7-48.

Canales, Arthur David. (2010b). "Youth and Eucharistic Worship," *Pastoral Liturgy*, 41 (4), 4-8.

Crawford, Marissa and Rossiter, Graham. (1996). "The Secular Spirituality of Youth: Implications for Religious Education," *British Journal of Religious Education*, 18 (3), 133-143.

Crawford, Marissa and Rossiter, Graham. (2004). "Teaching Wisdom: Religious Education and the Moral and Spiritual Development of Young People," *Journal of Christian Education*, 47 (2), 66-72.

Engebretson, Kathleen. (2004). "Teenage Boys, Spirituality, and Religion," *International Journal of Children's Spirituality*, 9 (3), 263-278.

Engebretson, Kathleen. (2006). "God's Got Your Back: Teenage Boys Talk About God," *International Journal of Children's Spirituality*, 11 (3): 329-345.

Manno, Bruno. (1979). "Distancing One's Self Religiously." *New Catholic World*, 222 September/October.

McQuillan, Paul. (2004). "Youth Spirituality-A Reality in Search of Expression," *Journal of Youth and Theology*, 3 (2), 8-25.

McQuillan, Paul. (2009). "Youth Ministry in a Changing World: The International Research Project on Youth Spirituality," *Journal of Youth Ministry*, 7 (2), 73-92.

Mehlman, Clement. (2000). "Practicing Spiritual Direction," *Pneuma*, 6 (2), 1-8.

Purpura, Joseph F. (2008). "Youth and Spiritual Direction," *Antiochian Orthodox Christian Archdiocese of North America*, pp. 1-3. http://www.antiochian.org/youth_spiritual_direction

White, David F. (2008). "Dialogue Toward a Practice of Discernment with Youth: A Response to Ketcham's Question of Capacity," *Journal of Youth Ministry*, 6 (2), 31-40.

Zagano, Phyllis. (2003). "Examen of Consciousness: Finding God in All Things," *Catholic Update*, (March 2003) 1-4.

## Books

Arnett, Jeffrey Jensen. (2002). *Readings on Adolescence and Emerging Adulthood.* Upper Saddle River, NJ: Prentice Hall.

Barron, Robert. (2002). *The Strangest Way: Walking the Christian Path.* Maryknoll, NY: Orbis Books.

Beck, Laura E. (1993). *Infants, Children, and Adolescents.* Boston, MA: Allyn and Bacon.

Bellah, Robert N. (1985). *Habits of the Heart.* Berkeley, CA: University of California Press.

Brueggemann, Walter. (1997). *The Bible Makes Sense.* Winona, MN: Saint Mary's Press.

Cavalletti, Sofia. (1992). *The Religious Potential of the Child: Experiencing Scripture and Liturgy with Young Children.* Chicago, IL: Liturgy Training Publications.

Cunningham, Lawrence S. and Keith J. Egan. (1996). *Christian Spirituality: Themes from the Tradition.* New York, NY: Paulist Press.

Delio, Ilia, O.S.F. (2004). *Franciscan Prayer.* Cincinnati, OH: Saint Anthony Messenger Press.

Delio, Ilia, O.S.F.. (2005). *The Humility of God: A Franciscan Perspective.* Cincinnati, OH: Saint Anthony Messenger Press.

East, Thomas. (2004). *Effective Practices for Dynamic Youth Ministry.* Winona, MN: St.

Mary's Press. East, Thomas. (2009). *Leadership for Catholic Youth Ministry: A Comprehensive Resource.* New London, CT: Twenty-Third Publications.

Freud, Anna. (1946). *The Ego and the Mechanism of Defense.* New York, NY: International Universities Press.

Lerner, Richard M. (2002). *Adolescence: Development, Diversity, Context, and Application.* Upper Saddle River, NJ: Prentice Hall.

Lindle, Jane C. (2005). *Affirming their Faith, Dispelling Old Myths: Ministry with Young Adolescents.* Winona, MN: Saint Mary's Press.

Lonergan, Bernard, J.F. (1958). *Insight: A Study of Human Understanding.* New York, NY: Harper & Row.

Lonergan, Bernard. J.F. (1972). *Method in Theology.* New York, NY: The Seabury Press.

McCarty, Robert J. (1994). *Survival in Youth Ministry.* Winona, MN: Saint Mary's Press.

# Bibliography

Montessori, Maria. (1911). *Spontaneous Activity in Education*, translated by Florence Simmons. New York, NY: Schocken Books.

Mueller, Walt. (2007). *Youth Culture 101*. Grand Rapids, MI: Youth Specialties.

Nemeck, Francis Kelly and Marie Theresa Coombs. (1993). *The Way of Spiritual Direction*. Collegeville, MN: The Liturgical Press.

Niebuhr, Richard H. (1951). *Christ and Culture*. New York, NY: Harper and Brothers.

Parrott, Less III. (2000). *Helping the Struggling Adolescent: A Guide to Thirty-Six Common Problems for Counselors, Pastors, and Youth Workers*. Grand Rapids, MI: Zondervan.

Parks, Sharon Daloz. (2000). *Big Questions, Worthy Dreams: Mentoring Young Adults in Their Search for Meaning, Purpose, and Faith*. San Francisco, CA: Jossey-Bass.

Pilarzyk, Daniel E. (1986). *Living in the Lord: The Building Blocks of Spirituality* Cincinnati, Ohio: Saint Anthony Messenger Press.

Rahner, Karl. (1978). *Foundations of Christian Faith*. New York, NY: Crossroads.

Rice, Philip F. and Kim Gale Dolgin. (2005). *The Adolescent: Development, Relationship, and Culture*, Eleventh Edition. Boston, MA: Pearson Education, Inc.

Shelton, Charles M., S.J. (1983). *Adolescent Spirituality: Pastoral Ministry for High School and College Youth*. Chicago, IL: Loyola University Press.

Strommen, Merton P. and Richard A. Hardel. (2000). *Passing on the Faith: A Radical New Model for Youth and Family Ministry*. Winona, MN: St. Mary's Press.

Smith, Christian and Melinda Lundquist Denton. (2005). *Soul Searching: The Religious and Spiritual Lives of American Teenagers*. New York, NY: Oxford University Press.

Tacey, David J. (2004). *The Spirituality Revolution: The Emergence of Contemporary Spirituality*. New York, NY: Brunner-Routledge.

Teilhard de Chardin, Pierre. (1960). *The Divine Milieu*. New York, NY: Harper.

White, David F. (2005). *Practicing Discernment with Youth: A Transformative Youth Ministry Approach*. Cleveland, OH: The Pilgrim Press.

Wright, Andrew. (2000). *Spirituality and Education*. London: Routledge-Falmer.

Yaconelli, Mark. (2005). *Growing Souls: Experiments in Contemplative Youth Ministry*. Grand Rapids, MI: Zondervan.

Yaconelli, Mark. (2006). *Contemplative Youth Ministry: Practicing the Presence of Jesus*. Grand Rapids, MI: Youth Specialties.

## Catholic Church Documents

Bishops' Committee on the Liturgy. (2004). *Thirty-One Questions on Adoration of the Blessed Sacrament*. Washington, DC: USCCB Publishing.

Congregation for Divine Worship. (1971). *General Instruction of the Liturgy of the Hours. In The Liturgy Documents, Volume Two: A Parish Resource with Commentary and Cumulative Index*. Chicago, IL: Liturgy Training Publications, pp. 260-313.

Congregation for Divine Worship. (1973). *Holy Communion and Worship of the Eucharist Outside Mass*. New York, NY: Catholic Book Publishing Company.

Congregation for the Clergy. (1997). *General Directory for Catechesis*. Washington, D.C.: United States Catholic Conference.

Department of Education. (1976). *A Vision of Youth Ministry*. Washington, D.C.: United States Catholic Conference.

Lumen Gentium. (1964). In Austin Flannery, O.P., edits, *Vatican Council II: The Conciliar and Post-Conciliar Documents, New Revised Study Edition 1992*. New York, NY: Costello Publishing Company, pp. 350-426.

National Conference of Catholic Bishops. (1997). *Renewing the Vision: A Framework for Catholic Youth Ministry*. Washington, DC: United States Catholic Conference.

National Federation for Catholic Youth Ministry. (1986). *The Challenge of Adolescent Catechesis: Maturing in Faith*. In Laurie Delgatto edits, *Catholic Youth Ministry: The Essential Documents*. Winona, MN: Saint Mary's Press, pp. 58-95.

National Federation for Catholic Youth Ministry. (1997). *From Age to Age: The Challenge of Worship with Adolescents*. In Laurie Delgatto edits, *Catholic Youth Ministry: The Essential Documents*. Winona, MN: Saint Mary's Press, pp. 24-57.

Pope Benedict XVI. (2010). "On the Occasion of the Twenty-Fifth Anniversary of the Inauguration of World Youth Day (March 28). http://www.vatican.va.holy_father/benedict_xvi.

Pope John Paul II. (1979). "Address at Saint Patrick's Cathedral." *Catholic News Service*, New York, NY: 3 October.

Pope John Paul II. (1980a). "Two Addresses to Youth: Homily in Boston." *The Catholic Mind*, 78 (January) 25-29.

Pope John Paul II. (1980b). "Homily in New York City." *The Catholic Mind*, 78 (January) 30-39.

Pope John Paul II. (1987). *Redemptoris Mater (The Mother of the Redeemer)*. Washington, DC: United States Catholic Conference.

Pope John Paul II. (1999). *Ecclesia in America: On the Encounter with the Living Jesus Christ, the Way to Conversion, Communion, and Solidarity in America* (The Church in America). Washington, DC: United States Catholic Conference.

Pope John Paul II. (2002). *Rosarium Virginis Mariae (On the Most Holy Rosary)*. Washington, DC: United States Catholic Conference.

Pope Paul VI. (1974). *Marialis Cultus (On the Cult of Mary)*. Washington, DC: United

Sacrosanctum Concilium. (1963). In Austin Flannery, O.P., edits, *Vatican Council II: The Conciliar and Post-Conciliar Documents, New Revised Study Edition 1992*. New York, NY: Costello Publishing Company, pp. 1-36.

United States Catholic Conference. (1986). *Prophetic Voices: The Document on the Process of the III Encuentro Nacional Hispano de Pastoral*. Washington, D.C.: USCC.

United States Conference of Catholic Bishops. (1997). *Catechism of the Catholic Church, Second Edition*. Washington, DC: USCCB Publishing.

United States Conference of Catholic Bishops. (2005). *Co-workers in the Vineyard of the Lord: A Resource for Guiding the Development of Lay Ecclesial Ministry*. Washington, DC: USCC Publishing.

## Essays or Chapters in Books

Aden, LeRoy. (2005). "Truth-telling." In Rodney J. Hunter edits, *Dictionary of Pastoral Care and Counseling* (Nashville, TN: Abingdon Press), pp. 1288-1289.

Aquinas, Thomas. (1948). "Of Adoration." *Summa Theologica*, translated by the Fathers of the English Dominican Province, Volume III, IIa, IIae, Question 84, Article 2, p. 1547. Westminster, MD: Christian Classics.

Augustine, Saint. (1986). "Sermon 272." In Daniel J. Sheerin edits, "O Taste and See: Eucharistic Instructions." *The Eucharist: Message of the Fathers of the Church*. Wilmington, Delaware: Michael Glazier Press, pp. 93-102.

Buckley, Michael J. (1993). "Discernment of Spirits." In Michael Downey edits, *The New Dictionary of Catholic Spirituality*. Collegeville, MN: The LiturgicalPress, pp. 274-281.

Carotta, Michael. (2002). "Revisiting Adolescent Catechesis," In *Adolescent Catechesis: Resources from the Living Light*. Washington, DC: USCCB Publishing, pp. 25-32.

Clarke, Corita. (1991). "An Integrated Spirituality," In Sharon Reed edits, *Spirituality: Access Guide to Youth Ministry*. New Rochelle, NY: Don Bosco Multimedia, pp. 49-59.

Driscoll, Jeremy. (2006). "Adoration of the Blessed Sacrament." *Book of Readings on the Eucharist*. Washington, DC: United States Conference of Catholic Bishops and Bishops' Committee on the Liturgy, pp. 85-92.

Freeman, Laurence. (1993). "Meditation," In Michael Downey edits, *The New Dictionary of Catholic Spirituality*. Collegeville, MN: The Liturgical Press, pp. 648-651.

Gratton, Carolyn. (1993). "Spiritual Direction," In Michael Downey edits, *The New Dictionary of Catholic Spirituality*. Collegeville, MN: The Liturgical Press, pp. 911-916.

Irwin, Kevin W. (1993). "Lectio Divina." In Michael Downey edits, *The New Dictionary of Catholic Spirituality*. Collegeville, MN: The Liturgical Press, p. 596.

Keating, Thomas. (1993). "Centering Prayer," In Michael Downey edits, *The New Dictionary of Catholic Spirituality*. Collegeville, MN: The Liturgical Press, pp. 138-139.

McBrien Richard P. (1995a). "Cardinal Virtues." In Richard P. McBrien edits, *Encyclopedia of Catholicism*. San Francisco, CA: Harper-San Francisco, pp. 227-228.

McBrien, Richard P. (1995b). "Theological Virtues." In Richard P. McBrien edits, *Encyclopedia of Catholicism*. San Francisco, CA: Harper-San Francisco, pp. 1249-1250.

McKenna, John H. (1990). "Theology of Adoration." In Peter E. Fink edits, *The New Dictionary of Theology*. Collegeville, MN: The Liturgical Press, pp. 25-28.

Reed, Sharon. (1991a). "A Spirituality Challenging Vision of Youth." In Sharon Reed edits, *Spirituality: Access Guide to Youth Ministry*. New Rochelle, NY: Don Bosco Multimedia, pp. 3-12.

Reed, Sharon. (1991b). "Directions for a Spirituality for Adolescents." In Sharon Reed edits, *Spirituality: Access Guide to Youth Ministry*. New Rochelle, NY: Don Bosco Multimedia, pp. 93-101.

# Bibliography

Reynolds, Sean. (2005). "The State of Catholic Adolescents." In Robert J. McCarty edits, *The Vision of Catholic Youth Ministry: Fundamentals, Theory, and Practice*. Winona, MN: Saint Mary's Press, pp. 41-55.

Rohde, Gregory. (1991). "Spiritual Direction with Adolescents." In Sharon Reed edits, *Spirituality: Access Guide to Youth Ministry*. New Rochelle, NY: Don Bosco Multimedia, pp. 171-181.

Sanabria, Tomás V. (2007). "Personal Religious Beliefs and Experiences." In Ken Johnson-Mondragón edits, *Pathways of Hope and Faith Among Hispanic Teens: Pastoral Reflections and Strategies Inspired by the National Study of Youth and Religion*. Stockton, CA: *Instituto Fe y Vida*, pp. 41-79.

Shannon, William H. (1993). "Contemplation and Contemplative Prayer," In Michael Downey edits, *The New Dictionary of Catholic Spirituality*. Collegeville, MN: The Liturgical Press, pp. 209-214.

Warren, Michael. (1987). "Understanding the Weekend format," In Michael Warren edits, *Readings and Resources in Youth Ministry*. Winona, MN: Saint Mary's Press, pp. 128-136.

Warren, Michael. (1991). "Twenty-Five Years of Youth Weekends: A Revised Appraisal." In Reynolds R. Ekstrom edits, *Retreats: Access Guides to Youth Ministry*. New Rochelle, NY: Don Bosco Multimedia, pp. 5-15.

# ENDNOTES

[1] Pope John Paul II, "The 1995 World Day of Prayer and Vocations"; located in *Renewing the Vision: A Framework for Catholic Youth Ministry*, Washington, DC: USCCB Publishing, 1997, p. 10.

[2] I am grateful to the following academic journals for allowing me to re-print and re-position some of the material that I wrote for them: *Emmanuel: Eucharistic Spirituality*, *International Journal of Children's Spirituality*, and *Journal of Youth Ministry*. For copies of the original work please see "Strengthening Eucharistic Spirituality in Adolescents," *Emmanuel: Eucharistic Spirituality*, Volume 115, Number 1 (January/February, 2009), pp. 9-23 (Emmanuel@blessedsacrament.com); "A Noble Quest: Cultivating Christian Spirituality in Catholic Adolescents and the Usefulness of 12 Pastoral Practices," *International Journal of Children's Spirituality*, Volume 14, Number 1 (Spring, 2009), pp. 63-77 (www.informaworld.com); "Addressing Catholic Adolescent Spirituality and Assessing Three Spiritual Practices for Young People in Catholic Youth Ministry," *Journal of Youth Ministry*, Volume 8, Number 2 (Spring, 2010), pp. 7-49 (www.aymeducators.org). I also want to thank the editors of those fine journals for granting permission to re-publish some of the contents of those articles: Rev. Paul Bernier, SSS, Cathy Ota, Ph.D. and Karin Beesley, and Mark W. Cannister, Ed.D.

[3] Jeffrey Jensen Arnett (2002), *Readings on Adolescence and Emerging Adulthood*, 2-3. Originally published by G. Stanley Hall (1904) *Adolescence: Its Psychology and Its Relation to Physiology, Anthropology, Sociology, Sex, Crime, Religion, and Education*, 513-589; D. Appleton and Company. G. Stanley Hall (1844-1924), rightly considered the founder of the scientific study of adolescence and adolescent psychology. His watershed two-volume work, published in 1904, sought to include every known fact concerning adolescence from biological development to religious matters. Hall presented adolescent life ranging from fourteen to twenty-four and studied teenagers as they had been portrayed throughout the centuries in literature, history, art, and biographies.

[4] I must acknowledge my own limitations; that is, I am not a professionally trained psychologist; however, I have studied adolescent behavior

and adolescence within the context of Christian theology and ministry, as well as worked in adolescent ministry for over twenty years in some capacity. At any rate, I am relying heavily on two sources for this particular section of the book: (1) Steven P. VandenAvond, Ph.D., Professor of Psychology, and Associate Academic Dean, University of Wisconsin at Green Bay, who is both friend and former colleague and has given valuable advice, coaching, and mentoring about the psychological and developmental issues surrounding adolescents and adolescent behavior and developmental theories; and (2) Charles M. Shelton, S.J., and his book *Adolescent Spirituality: Pastoral Ministry for High School and College Youth*, in particular chapter three titled, "Adolescence, Developmental Theory, and Spirituality," pp. 29-120.

[5] The data collected in the study actually involved twelfth graders from the Seventh Day Adventist Church and American twelfth graders involved in at-risk behavior; therefore the data may be somewhat one-sided; it nevertheless demonstrates that religious values do impact and influence teenage behavior. The exact data can be found in Merton P. Strommen and Richard A. Hardel (2000), *Passing on the Faith: A Radical New Model for Youth and Family Ministry*, Winona, MN: Saint Mary's Press.

[6] Department of [Catholic] Education, *A Vision of Youth Ministry*, Washington, DC: United States Catholic Conference, 1976, pp. 6-7.

[7] Mark Yaconelli has written two recent books that encompass adolescent spirituality: *Growing Souls: Experiments in Contemplative Youth Ministry* (2005) and *Contemplative Youth Ministry: Practicing the Presence of Jesus* (2006). Both books are the result of Youth Ministry and Spirituality Project (1997-2004) funded by the Lilly Endowment. Despite the books' new appeal to Protestant and Evangelical Christians, Yaconelli uses almost exclusively Roman Catholic writers, traditions, and rituals for the findings in his books (but offers little, if any, acknowledgment to the Catholic Church and its rich heritage of contemplative prayer). Nevertheless, Catholic youth ministers will feel comfortable integrating these spiritual practices into their faith formation. For instance, Yaconelli offers strategies to help adolescents become more spiritually attuned to God such as: (1) *Lectio Divina* or "holy reading," a Catholic monastic spiritual discipline started by Saint Benedict of Nursia (480-547), which has a basic structure of silence, scripture reading, meditation, oration, and contemplation; (2) Centering Prayer, which is focusing on thoughts, words, and images, and is a medieval spiritual discipline attributed to Catholic mystics and saints Julia of Norwich (1342-1420), Teresa of Avila (1515-1582), and John of the Cross (1542-1591), and has had contemporary resurgence and following from Catholic Cistercian priests Thomas Keating, William Menninger, and Basil Pennington; (3) the Awareness Examen or Examination of Consciousness is taken directly for the Catholic priest and founder of the Society of Jesus Order (Jesuits) Saint Ignatius of Loyola (1491-1556), whereby Ignatius called it *The Spiritual Exercises*. It is an exercise of growth in discernment and awareness usually in

the form of a 30-day, 15-day, or 7-day retreat; and (4) the Liturgy of Discernment, which is a reinterpretation of Catholic Jesuit priest and psychologist Matthew Linn and his brother, Catholic psychologist and lay minister Dennis Linn, and his wife Sheila Linn and their book *Sleeping with Bread* (Paulist Press, 1995), which integrates all the previous three ways of praying into an easy-to-use recipe for youth ministers to follow involving ritual: relating, receiving, ruminating, reflecting, responding, and returning (Yaconelli, 2005, pp. 259-272). All these spiritual practices that Yaconelli suggests originated in the Catholic Church and were formally designed to bolster adult spirituality, *not* adolescent spirituality; consequently, the task for youth ministers is to implement spiritual practices that connect with young people in ways that engage them and empower their spirituality.

[8] Christian Smith and Melinda L. Denton's investigation and evaluation was not based on just a few sample interviews. Rather, their evaluation was based on a national representative sample of hundreds of Catholic teenagers who were questioned over the telephone about their religious and spiritual beliefs. There were also face-to-face interviews, which were also a nationally representative sub-sample of the original teenagers that had completed the telephone survey. For more information, see Smith and Denton (2005), *Soul Searching: The Religious and Spiritual Lives of American Teenagers* (New York, NY: Oxford University Press) pp. 193-217. There is an issue of the questions that were posed to Catholic youth and their understanding of the questions asked and whether those questions rightly reflect Catholic jargon and Catholic culture. At any rate, the findings are still rather alarming.

[9] For Smith and Denton, the "devoted" adolescents included only those who (1) believe in God, (2) attend religious services weekly or more, (3) say that their faith is very or extremely important in their lives, (4) regularly participate in religious youth ministries, (5) feel very or extremely close to God, and (6) pray and read the Bible regularly (pp. 108-114).

[10] "Stations of the Cross" refers to the depiction of the final hours of Jesus of Nazareth and the devotion commemorating the Passion. The tradition as chapel devotion began with Saint Francis of Assisi and extended throughout Western Christianity in the medieval period. "Stations of the Cross " are less often observed in the Anglican and Lutheran traditions. "Stations of the Cross" may be celebrated at any time, but are most commonly experienced during the liturgical seasons of Advent, Lent, and the Triduum (Maundy Thursday, Good Friday, and Holy Saturday).

[11] Pope Paul VI, *On Christian Joy*, Apostolic Exhortation, (Washington, D.C.: United States Catholic Conference, 1975) 30-31.

[12] The term "comprehensive" is extremely important for Catholic youth ministry in the United States. "The buzzword in Catholic youth ministry circles over the past ten years is *comprehensive*, which describes a systematic and integrated approach to youth ministry outlined in *Renewing*

*the Vision* and is the preferred approach to doing ministry with adolescents" (Canales, 2007; p. 59). Moreover, comprehensive youth ministry stresses the faith, moral, and spiritual development of adolescents while incorporating young people into the mission and ministry of Jesus Christ. Furthermore, "comprehensive Catholic youth ministry means that youth ministers and adolescents alike become increasingly aware that the Catholic faith is for them-all of it-not only selective parts. That is to suggest, ministry to adolescents ideally moves beyond a ministry that focuses on 'my youth group' or 'my parish' to embrace a larger ecclesiastical worldview: universal church, preferential option for the poor, family, multiculturalism, intergenerational, diocese, etc." (Canales, 2007; p. 60). Therefore, comprehensive Catholic youth ministry situates ministry to adolescents in a larger pastoral framework and context beyond the boundaries of a particular congregation.

[13] The official Rite of Eucharistic Exposition and Benediction has four parts: (1) exposition, (2) adoration, (3) benediction, and (4) reposition. For more information see, *Holy Communion and Worship of the Eucharist Outside Mass*, 1973; no. 93-100.

[14] Perhaps a topic for a subsequent book could be written because there are some potential pastoral pitfalls and liturgical dangers to pay attention to when celebrating Eucharistic Exposition and Benediction in youth ministry settings. Since Eucharistic Exposition and Benediction is an official liturgical rite of the Catholic Church, it is not a question of *why* parishes, youth ministries, and the People of God partake in Eucharistic adoration, but *how* those parishes, youth ministries, and people participate in Eucharistic adoration. It is the *how* that would make for an excellent and beneficial investigation. For more on the pastoral pitfalls and liturgical dangers of celebrating Eucharistic Exposition and Benediction apart from the Sunday Assembly see Arthur David Canales, (2010), "Youth and Eucharistic Worship, *Pastoral Liturgy*, 41 (4), 4-8; Arthur David Canales, (2011), "What's All the Fuss About? The Overzealousness of Celebrating Eucharistic Adoration Apart from the Sunday Assembly," *Chicago Studies*, 49 (3), 318-331.

[15] The term "reserved sacrament" usually refers to and describes the practice of brining from the tabernacle previously consecrated Eucharistic elements of bread (and wine, if available and permitted, although current liturgical rites for Holy Communion outside Mass restrict the elements to the consecrated bread). These elements have been part of the sacrifice, memorial, offering, thanksgiving, and dining of another assembly's table-friendship and meal-companionship; now they are being used for either a new assembly's act of receiving Holy Communion in the context of a non-Eucharistic liturgy. Traditionally, receiving the reserved sacrament, except for people in restricted situations (e.g., in prison, or confined to bed, or unable to join the community because of war, distance, religious persecution, and the like), is not sound liturgical theology or practice because Catholics and other Christians who are able are mandated to gather around the altar and eat and

drink from the table, not the tabernacle. For more information see Gerard Austin, "Communion Services: A Break with Tradition?" in *The Fountain of Life*, ed. Gerard Austin (Washington, DC: The Pastoral Press, 1991) pp. 199-215; James Dallen, *The Dilemma of Priestless Sundays* (Chicago, IL: Liturgy Training Publications, 1994); Arthur David Canales, *Toward a Theological, Liturgical, and Pastoral Understanding of Sunday Parish Worship with Deacon and Lay Presiders* (Washington, DC: The Catholic University of America, unpublished doctoral dissertation, 1996).

[16] The theme of the retreat could be the "Source and Summit" or the "Bread of Life." The retreat could focus on various topics pertaining to Sunday Eucharist such as the significance of Sunday, the Eucharistic narratives in the Gospels, the Eucharistic Prayers, the primacy of the gathered assembly, and/or the connection between Liturgy of the Hours and Sunday Eucharist. All of these themes should help highlight the paramount importance that Sunday Eucharist has for Catholic identity and Catholic spirituality, which are interdependent with Catholic ministry and life. Sometime during the retreat, Eucharistic Exposition and Benediction could be observed after Sunday Eucharist. If the retreat center is deemed officially Catholic (diocesan retreat center) and there already exists an established sacred space such as an officially consecrated chapel, then midnight Mass could be celebrated and immediately following Mass, Eucharistic Exposition and Benediction could be observed. Or perhaps, on Sunday morning before the conclusion of the retreat, and after the celebration of Sunday Eucharist, Eucharistic exposition and benediction could be observed. In both scenarios, Eucharistic adoration takes place within the context of Sunday Eucharist, but also after a healthy discussion of the Eucharistic theology (during the retreat) and is part of the culminating worship experience within the retreat.

[17] The youth could assemble and celebrate Sunday Eucharist at the diocesan cathedral and immediately following Mass; Eucharistic Exposition and Benediction could be provided (with approval of the cathedral rector). After adoration, the young people would go out and feed the homeless population, or volunteer at a soup kitchen, or travel with *Mobil Loaves and Fishes or Meals on Wheels* (again this would have to be pre-arranged by the youth minister or adult chaperone). After a few of hours of service and outreach in the community, there should be a debriefing about the entire experience: Mass, Eucharistic veneration, and service project. This activity clearly links adoration with action and could easily be termed "Eucharistic Evangelization" because it models a Eucharistic ecclesiology that is rooted in the Gospel values of service and social justice. This type of Eucharistic celebration clearly leads to personal and communal transformation.

[18] Augustine of Hippo, Sermon, 272. Located in "O Taste and See: Eucharistic Instructions." In Daniel J. Sheerin edits, *The Eucharist: Message of the Fathers of the Church* (Wilmington, DE: Michael Glazier Press, 1986) p. 95.

# Endnotes

[19] Pope John Paul II, "Youth Sent to Proclaim True Liberation," World Youth Day, 1995, Philippines. This quote is an excerpt from *Renewing the Vision: A Framework for Catholic Youth Ministry* (1997) 2.

[20] United States Catholic Conference, *Prophetic Voices: The Document on the Process of the III Encuentro Nacional Hispano de Pastoral*, Washington, D.C.: USCC, 1986, p. 11.

[21] Although "psychologically and socially adolescents are typically broken into three categories: younger adolescents 11 to 14 years of age, middle adolescents 15 to 18 years of age, and older adolescents 1 – 22 years of age" (Canales, 2005a, p. 4), this article reflects pastoral ministry with Catholic middle adolescents.

[22] For a more thorough reading, see David F. White (2005), *Practicing Discernment with Youth: A Transformative Youth Ministry Approach*, pp. 88-199, where he gives fuller detail of the fourfold drama merely listed here and will provide the reader with much valuable information and insight.

[23] For more information on Eucharistic Exposition and Benediction of the Blessed Sacrament and the involvement of Catholic youth, see Arthur David Canales (2009), "*Strengthening Eucharistic Spirituality in Adolescents*," *Emmanuel: Eucharistic Spirituality*, 115 (1): 9-23.

[24] The term "Blessed Sacrament" is sacred for Catholics. The Blessed Sacrament implies that a previously consecrated communion host (which for Catholics is the body of Christ, who is wholly present in the communion host) and is reserved and placed in a position of prominence. The Blessed Sacrament is usually placed in a Monstrance that is set apart in a designated liturgical space typically referred to as a "Blessed Sacrament Chapel" in a local parish or regional church for the sole purpose of prayer, meditation, and contemplation.

[25] Pope Benedict XVI, "On the Occasion of the Twenty-Fifth Anniversary of the Inauguration of World Youth Day (March 28, 2010): http://www.vatican.va.holy_father/benedict_xvi.

[26] Pope John Paul II, *The Church in America: On the Encounter with the Living Christ, The Way to Conversion and Solidarity in America*, Washington, DC: United States Catholic Conference, 1999.

# ABOUT THE AUTHOR

Arthur David Canales, D.Min., ("Art") is a freelance Catholic theologian, adolescent ministry scholar, professional speaker, and recognized author who brings the gift of adolescent catechetical training to parishes and dioceses. Art has diverse ministry experiences and and empowers young people and adults alike in the richness of Catholic theology by intersecting them with comprehensive Catholic youth ministry. Moreover, he is one of the very few people to write about Catholic youth ministry to the theological academy in scholarly articles which help to bring comprehensive youth ministry to the forefront of the Church's mission.

Dr. Canales received a baccalaureate degree from Florida International University (Miami, Florida), Master of Arts degrees from University of Miami (Coral Gables, Florida), Master of Divinity degree from The Catholic University of America (Washington, D.C.), Master of Liturgical Studies degree from the University of Notre Dame (South Bend, Indiana), and a Doctor of Ministry degree from The Catholic University of America (Washington, D.C.) with an emphasis in pastoral theology and liturgical and sacramental theology. His doctoral dissertation is titled, *Toward a Theological, Liturgical, and Pastoral Understanding of Sunday Parish Worship with Deacon and/or Lay Presiders* (CUA Press).

Art has previously served as a **parish coordinator of youth ministry** (Miami; Washington, D.C.; Beltsville, Maryland), **college campus minister** (Coral Gables, Florida), and as a **diocesan director of youth, young adult ministry, and campus ministry** (Austin, Texas). He has also served as an associate adjunct professor of theology at Saint Thomas University (Miami, Florida), Saint Edward's University (Austin, Texas), as an **associate professor of theology and ministry** at Silver Lake College of the Holy Family (Manitowoc, Wisconsin), and is also the creator of and an instructor for the Diocese of Austin's Youth Ministry Certification Program. Art has also been part of a national Hispanic/Latino Adolescent and Family "think tank," the *Instituto Fe y Vida* (Stockton, California). In addition, Canales served three years on the Board of Directors to Catholic Charities of Central Texas (Austin, Texas).

Art's theological writings are prolific, diverse, and numerous. He has written over 40 pastoral-theological educational essays for the *Herald Times Reporter* newspaper in Manitowoc, Wisconsin (2000-2006). He has written for various pastoral and scholarly publications: *Pastoral Music* (1996), *Ministry* (2000), *The Living Light* (2002), *Journal of Pentecostal Theology* (2003), *Journal of the Association of Franciscan Colleges and Universities* (2004), *Catechumenate* (2005), *Apuntes Reflexiones Teológicas* (2005), *Religious Education* (2006), *Journal of the American Academy of Religion* (2006), *New Theology Review* (2007), *Stewardship Reflections* (2008), *Emmanuel: Eucharistic Spirituality* (2009, 2010), *International Journal of Children's Spirituality* (2009), *Journal of Youth Ministry* (2010), *Pastoral Liturgy* (2010), *Chicago Studies* (2011), and *Verbum Incarnatum* (2011). Art is co-author of **Keeping the Cup Full: Financial Stewardship for Teens and Young Adults (2008, 2009) and** *Beating the Credit Game: Financial and Money Management for Teens and Young Adults* **(2008, 2009). He is also author of** *Models for Youth Ministry: A Comprehensive Catholic Approach to Adolescent Ministry* (forthcoming).

Art is a sought-after keynote speaker and workshop presenter and has given workshops, seminars, and keynote presentations in over 30 dioceses around the country. He speaks on numerous pastoral and catechetical issues, but especially topics surrounding adolescents, Christology, discipleship, spirituality, stewardship, and youth ministry.

Dr. Art Canales can help empower and equip your parish youth ministry in the following areas:

    (1) Adult Catechist Training for Teenagers
    (2) Spiritual Direction Training
    (3) Adolescent & Adult Leadership Development
    (4) Pastoral Care & Counseling Training
    (5) Youth Ministry Certification
    (6) Various Ministry Seminars
    (7) Workshops in Liturgy & Sacraments
    (8) Theological Presentations
    (9) Conference Keynote Addresses

For more information on bringing Art to work with your adult youth leaders, youth core leaders, and/or with overall catechetical training and formation, including parish missions, retreats, various ministry workshops, theological presentations, and keynote addresses please e-mail him at:

artcanales@yahoo.com